S0-BCV-128

XML
FOR
DUMMIES®

Quick Reference

by Mariva H. Aviram

IDG Books Worldwide, Inc.
An International Data Group Company

Foster City, CA ✦ Chicago, IL ✦ Indianapolis, IN ✦ New York, NY

XML For Dummies® Quick Reference

Published by
IDG Books Worldwide, Inc.
An International Data Group Company
919 E. Hillsdale Blvd.
Suite 400
Foster City, CA 94404
www.idgbooks.com (IDG Books Worldwide Web site)
www.dummies.com (Dummies Press Web site)

Library of Congress Catalog Card No.: 98-85374

ISBN: 0-7645-0383-9

Printed in the United States of America

10 9 8 7 6 5 4 3 2 1

1P/QY/QV/ZY/IN

Distributed in the United States by IDG Books Worldwide, Inc.

Distributed by Macmillan Canada for Canada; by Transworld Publishers Limited in the United Kingdom; by IDG Norge Books for Norway; by IDG Sweden Books for Sweden; by Woodslane Pty. Ltd. for Australia; by Woodslane Enterprises Ltd. for New Zealand; by Longman Singapore Publishers Ltd. for Singapore, Malaysia, Thailand, and Indonesia; by Simron Pty. Ltd. for South Africa; by Toppan Company Ltd. for Japan; by Distribuidora Cuspide for Argentina; by Livraria Cultura for Brazil; by Ediciencia S.A. for Ecuador; by Addison-Wesley Publishing Company for Korea; by Ediciones ZETA S.C.R. Ltda. for Peru; by WS Computer Publishing Corporation, Inc., for the Philippines; by Unalis Corporation for Taiwan; by Contemporanea de Ediciones for Venezuela; by Computer Book & Magazine Store for Puerto Rico; by Express Computer Distributors for the Caribbean and West Indies. Authorized Sales Agent: Anthony Rudkin Associates for the Middle East and North Africa.

For general information on IDG Books Worldwide's books in the U.S., please call our Consumer Customer Service department at 800-762-2974. For reseller information, including discounts and premium sales, please call our Reseller Customer Service department at 800-434-3422.

For information on where to purchase IDG Books Worldwide's books outside the U.S., please contact our International Sales department at 650-655-3200 or fax 650-655-3295.

For information on foreign language translations, please contact our Foreign & Subsidiary Rights department at 650-655-3021 or fax 650-655-3281.

For sales inquiries and special prices for bulk quantities, please contact our Sales department at 650-655-3200 or write to the address above.

For information on using IDG Books Worldwide's books in the classroom or for ordering examination copies, please contact our Educational Sales department at 800-434-2086 or fax 817-251-8174.

For press review copies, author interviews, or other publicity information, please contact our Public Relations department at 650-655-3000 or fax 650-655-3299.

For authorization to photocopy items for corporate, personal, or educational use, please contact Copyright Clearance Center, 222 Rosewood Drive, Danvers, MA 01923, or fax 978-750-4470.

About the Author

An active Internet user since 1988 and a Web user since 1994, **Mariva Hannah Aviram** (not just a palindrome, but a real name) possesses fond memories of the "good old days" of the Net, when it was commercial-free and was enjoyed only by students and professional nerds. Mariva has provided technical consultation to a variety of corporate clients and has written articles and coauthored books on topics pertaining to the Internet. Written works include articles for CNET, *NetscapeWorld*'s "Webmaster Q&A" column, and a book and software product for Microsoft Press.

During nonworking time, Mariva turns off the computer to play or listen to music, watch films, cook, read, write, make crafts, play with the cats, and spend time in the great outdoors. You can find more information, including a background on the palindromic name, at Mariva's home page: www.mariva.com.

ABOUT IDG BOOKS WORLDWIDE

John Kilcullen
CEO
IDG Books Worldwide, Inc.

Steven Berkowitz
President and Publisher
IDG Books Worldwide, Inc.

Eighth Annual Computer Press Awards ≥1992

Ninth Annual Computer Press Awards ≥1993

Tenth Annual Computer Press Awards ≥1994

Eleventh Annual Computer Press Awards ≥1995

Dedication

To Boo.

Acknowledgments

Many thanks to Mary Bednarek for the opportunity to write this book. I'd also like to thank the staff members at IDG Books: Senior Acquisitions Editor Jill Pisoni, Copy Editor Ted Cains, and Project Editor Bill Helling. I owe a large debt of gratitude to my project editor, Robert Wallace, for his patience, professionalism, and kindness. I also want to thank Technical Editor Liam Quin of Groveware, Inc., for his expert eye.

I can't thank my agent and good friend, Janna Raye Custer, enough for her professionalism and support.

I extend my personal thanks to my family, especially Amittai Aviram, Ari Aviram, Sandy Aviram, Steven Aviram, Blake Gilson, and Ayala Abramsky and her family, and to my friends and associates whose support I always appreciate: Sarah Aminoff, Caroline Barlerin, Geoff Duncan, Rebecca Eisenberg, Patrick Fitzgerald, Trisha Gorman, Julia Kay, Helen Price, Gretchen Primack, Jennie Rose, Anne Ryder and John Brobst, and Fred Wobus.

This list wouldn't be complete without special thanks to Eric Wagner. Thank you for everything.

Publisher's Acknowledgments

We're proud of this book; please register your comments through our IDG Books Worldwide Online Registration Form located at: http://my2cents.dummies.com.

Some of the people who helped bring this book to market include the following:

Acquisitions, Editorial, and Media Development

Project Editor: Robert H. Wallace

Senior Acquisitions Editor: Jill Pisoni

Copy Editors: Ted Cains, Elizabeth Netedu Kuball

Technical Editor: Liam Quin

Editorial Manager: Colleen Rainsberger, Leah P. Cameron

Editorial Assistants: Darren Meiss, Donna Love

Production

Associate Project Coordinator: Tom Missler

Layout and Graphics: Lou Boudreau, Maridee V. Ennis, Angela F. Hunckler, Jane E. Martin, Drew R. Moore, Brent Savage, Kate Snell

Proofreaders: Kelli Botta, Michelle Croninger, Janet M. Withers

Indexer: Sherry Massey

General and Administrative

IDG Books Worldwide, Inc.: John Kilcullen, CEO; Steven Berkowitz, President and Publisher

IDG Books Technology Publishing: Brenda McLaughlin, Senior Vice President and Group Publisher

Dummies Technology Press and Dummies Editorial: Diane Graves Steele, Vice President and Associate Publisher; Mary Bednarek, Director of Acquisitions and Product Development; Kristin A. Cocks, Editorial Director

Dummies Trade Press: Kathleen A. Welton, Vice President and Publisher; Kevin Thornton, Acquisitions Manager

IDG Books Production for Dummies Press: Beth Jenkins Roberts, Production Director; Cindy L. Phipps, Manager of Project Coordination, Production Proofreading, and Indexing; Kathie S. Schutte, Supervisor of Page Layout; Shelley Lea, Supervisor of Graphics and Design; Debbie J. Gates, Production Systems Specialist; Robert Springer, Supervisor of Proofreading; Debbie Stailey, Special Projects Coordinator; Tony Augsburger, Supervisor of Reprints and Bluelines; Leslie Popplewell, Media Archive Coordinator

Dummies Packaging and Book Design: Patti Crane, Packaging Specialist; Kavish + Kavish, Cover Design

♦

The publisher would like to give special thanks to Patrick J. McGovern, without whom this book would not have been possible.

♦

Contents at a Glance

Table of Contents

How to Use This Book

So, you need a quick and ready reference book that covers all the important stuff about the new Extensible Markup Language (XML)? Well, you're holding the right book in your hands. And you can do anything you want with this book, as long as you don't lose it. Why? Because in *XML For Dummies Quick Reference*, you find everything you need to develop working XML DTDs and documents: tools and software, the rules of XML as defined by the XML Specification, proper syntax for all the types of declarations, the difference between logical and physical structure, and more.

This book is chock-full of information, but that doesn't mean you have to read through it from the beginning to the end. If you need to look up information on a particular topic, simply find the section devoted to that topic. Each section is a small, but complete, chunk of information, so you don't have to read a whole chapter or an entire book to find the exact syntax that you need or a helpful example of XML code.

Keep in mind that this is a convenient reference-type of book, and not an exhaustive source of information on XML. If you'd like to study XML and its associated applications in more depth, please consult the larger companion book, *XML For Dummies*, by Ed Tittel, Norbert Mikula, and Ramesh Chandak (IDG Books Worldwide, Inc.).

How This Book Is Organized

This book has six parts and two appendixes, each of which contains a number of sections that are organized alphabetically within the part or appendix. To find information on a specific topic, consider the general area that the topic would be classified under, and then look in the appropriate part or appendix. For example, to find information on declaring attributes, look in Part IV: Logical Structures, check under the heading "Attributes," and look for the subheading "Attribute-list declarations." Some alternative ways to find the information that you need include scanning the table of contents to see how the parts are organized, looking up a keyword in the index, or looking up a definition in the Techie Talk glossary.

The six parts and two appendixes of this book are organized by subject matter, as follows:

Part I: Getting to Know XML

If you need a refresher on the basics of XML, here's a good place to start. Part I contains information about XML itself, applications for XML DTDs and documents, using existing DTDs and creating new ones, information about the XML Specification, and lots of tools and software.

Part II: The XML Specification

The rules and regulations of XML — that is, how XML works and what is and isn't allowed — are outlined by the official XML Specification. The XML Specification, governed and hosted by the World Wide Web Consortium, was written — and is periodically updated — by a number of volunteers specializing in programming languages and Internet technology. In this part, you can learn about the XML Specification in more depth, including the difference between logical and physical structure; the notation and syntax of XML Specification rules; and literals, names, and tokens.

Part III: Designing an XML DTD

The document type definition (DTD) is as essential to XML as a list of ingredients to a recipe. In Part III, you find information on characters and character data, designing a DTD, validity and well-formedness, designing certain key types of markup and declarations, and the all-important white space.

Part IV: Logical Structures

This part represents one side of the XML equation: logical structure. Logical structure and structures involve, well, the logical organization of an XML DTD and document. In Part IV, you can look up instructions, syntaxes, and examples for attributes, conditional sections, elements, and markup tags. This part is very useful when taken in conjunction with Part V: Physical Structures.

Part V: Physical Structures

Part V represents the flip side of the XML equation, an important complement to Part IV: Logical Structures. As with logical structure, physical structure is an important concept in XML. This part provides you with the breakdown of what you need to employ the concept of physical structure: characters, character encoding schemes, notations, and entities — including the document entity, internal and external entities, parsed and unparsed entities, parameter entities, and predefined entities.

Part VI: Implementing XML

If you're ready to take the XML plunge, you might want to turn directly to Part VI. Here you find useful tips on implementing XML DTDs, documents, and systems. The section on applications for XML gives you some options for setting up XML functionality within your organization. If you've come from a background of SGML, or have been using SGML-compliant documents and systems, you definitely want to check out the section on SGML and XML. You can also find handy tips on testing your DTDs and documents in this part.

Appendix: XML Resources and Future Developments

You need more information? The Appendix contains a convenient list of informational resources on XML. Resources include a number of Web sites, books, publications, and other sources of XML-related material. Pay special attention to the list of Web sites, because often the Web is the best source of up-to-date information.

As with most other technology, XML isn't static. If you're even a little bit interested in the world of XML, you're probably aware that there are constantly new developments with XML, XML-related specifications, and XML software. I didn't have enough room to cover peripherally related XML topics in this book, but you can get more information about them in the appendix. Here you can find out about Extensible Style Language (XSL), the XML Linking Specification (XLL), metadata, the relationship between Java and XML, public style-sheet specifications, and XML used in and with scripting languages.

Techie Talk

Techie Talk is the glossary — an alphabetical listing of XML terms used throughout this book. The glossary is a convenient tool for finding out what terms like *DTD*, *parameter entity*, *Unicode*, *diacritic*, and *well-formed* mean.

What You Need to Know

I wrote *XML For Dummies Quick Reference* with the assumption that you already have a certain amount of technical skill and knowledge under your belt. XML is a tricky subject — and not generally recommended for technical novices — so having the basic requirements before you jump in is important.

You need to have some basic skill and experience with computer technology. Because XML is an open-systems and platform-independent specification, you can choose to work on any platform, such as Windows, Macintosh, or UNIX. Whichever platform you work on doesn't matter as long as you have a working familiarity with it, such as knowing how to organize files and directories or folders, install new software, and run a variety of applications.

XML was designed for use on the Web, so you should be comfortable with a variety of Internet technology and specifications, including the World Wide Web and HTML. Although it's not totally necessary, familiarity with some of the popular scripting languages used on the Web, such as Perl and JavaScript, can be very helpful.

If you have experience with a programming language, you may find it very helpful when learning XML. Although XML isn't exactly a programming language, the way C/C++ and Java are, it is a *markup language* — that is, a language that you use to design the markup used in documents — and you can benefit greatly from understanding general programming and syntactical concepts.

XML is a subset of SGML, so any familiarity with SGML is a big plus when learning XML. In fact, if you've studied or used SGML before, picking up XML will be a breeze.

Conventions Used in This Book

I use a number of conventions in this book that clarify the context of the information and also demonstrate the syntactical constructs of XML.

Fonts and text

Throughout this book you may notice that most of the text is plain, such as the way it appears in this sentence. Some of the text appears in a different font to differentiate or emphasize it. Words that are *italicized* indicate a technical term with an accompanying definition; the italics indicate the first instance of the term within the most relevant section. Words that appear in monofont are a piece of XML code. For example, the next sentence contains both a term and tiny pieces — in this case, single characters — of XML code:

Literal data is any quoted string that doesn't contain the double quotes (") or apostrophes (') as delimiters for that string.

A piece of code that is separated from the text, as in a rule taken from the XML Specification, a demonstration of proper syntax, or an example of XML code, looks like this:

```
<?XML version="1.0"?>
```

Sometimes, you find italics within the code to show that certain terms are variables — or placeholders for customized code that you input yourself — and are not part of the literal code. A section of code that includes a variable looks like this:

```
<!DOCTYPE rootElementName SYSTEM
    "filename.dtd">
```

In this example, rootElementName and filename.dtd are placeholders for actual code that you include. This convention makes it convenient for you to copy the syntax of the code that you need and input the rest in the right places.

Syntactical conventions

Parts II through VI contain sections that explain various constructs and methods in XML. Many of these sections include the relevant grammatical instructions — called *rules* — from the XML Specification. Part II details the specific nature of the XML Specification and shows how the notation and syntax of the rules work; however, if you want to go directly to another part, you need to be familiar with some of the syntactical conventions first.

All the rules of the XML Specification conform to Extended Backus-Naur Form (EBNF) notation, which looks like this:

```
symbol ::= expression
```

This syntax contains the following parts:

+ symbol refers to the name given to a particular rule.

+ : : = is the delimiter separating the symbol from the expression.

+ expression refers to the definition of the symbol, or what the symbol is instructed to do.

Each rule in the grammar defines one symbol. In some of the expressions (the right side of the : : =), you find the following constructs:

Construct	Appearance	Purpose
The logical "or"	|	The logical "or," or pipe, separates mutually exclusive parameter choices and indicates that exactly one of the choices must be used.
angle brackets	< and >	The left-angle bracket and the right-angle bracket (often referred to as "less-than" and "greater-than" signs) are used in pairs to enclose a piece of markup or a tag.
parentheses	(and)	Open and closed parentheses are used in pairs to enclose a section of code whose function precedes the rest of the code or is grouped together syntactically.
square brackets	[and]	The square brackets are used to contain a variety of options, such as a range of characters. Square brackets are also used to set apart well-formedness and validity constraints from the rest of an XML Specification rule.

Meet the Cast of Icons

When you read about a particular XML topic, you may run across a term or concept that relates to a different topic. The Cross-Reference icon sends you to the appropriate chapters or parts in the big book on this topic, *XML For Dummies.* That book contains more detailed information on the term or concept. (You can think of the Cross-Reference icon as the paper version of a link on a Web page.)

This icon accompanies useful examples of XML code. You can either use the example to better understand the related XML concept, or you can borrow and experiment with it in your own XML application.

The Syntax icon indicates the straightforward grammatical template for implementing a particular line or piece of XML code, such as a declaration or a set of tags.

 This icon indicates a tidbit of information that can make your life with XML a little easier.

 Of all the icons, this is one you should pay attention to. The Warning! bomb indicates some information that can help you prevent problems, such as the XML processor triggering fatal errors.

 The Weirdness icon points out unexpected things you should watch out for in the course of your XML implementation, such as exceptions to general rules or functions that are illogical or strange.

 This icon provides the URL of a Web site that you can peruse for more detailed information on a related topic or about an organization that provides technical information or specifications.

Author Contact Information

I hope that you find this reference useful in your XML endeavors. I'm sure that you'll use XML to create a variety of new and useful DTDs, documents, and publishing systems. You might even use XML to come up with unique solutions for specific publishing or programming problems. I'd love to hear your comments and suggestions. Please feel free to contact me by e-mail at mariva@mariva.com. You may also view my Web page at www.mariva.com.

Part 1

Getting to Know XML

If you've been working with a variety of document formats and data-management systems, you may have wished for a tool or a standard to bridge together the differing technologies. XML has the potential to become such a bridge. XML combines the power of SGML with the network-optimization of HTML to create an excellent new standard for document exchange. XML is also compatible with a variety of programming languages, Web data formats, and Internet protocols. After studying and using XML for a while, you may reach the conclusion that it's the best thing since pizza.

Although XML has only been developed recently, the interest from the Internet and programming communities has been phenomenal. As soon as the idea for XML became public, a number of individuals and software vendors began incorporating XML-friendly specifications into their products, writing articles and documentation on XML, and releasing their own XML software.

This part offers an introduction into XML, its relationship to SGML and HTML, and available tools and software.

In this part . . .

- ✔ Becoming familiar with the basic concepts of XML

- ✔ Discovering XML applications

- ✔ Understanding the basic difference between DTDs and documents

- ✔ Finding out about the different types of XML tools and software

- ✔ Brainstorming on the possibilities of XML

- ✔ Understanding both the differences and the similarities between XML and SGML

- ✔ Understanding the difference between XML and HTML

About XML

Extensible Markup Language (XML) is a recent development in the world of Web-related specifications. Lots of Web and intranet developers are paying attention to XML and its speedy evolution, because it represents tremendous potential for solving a variety of document-system problems and for easily and efficiently bridging document systems to other types of computer systems.

XML is an international standard for electronic document exchange developed by a group of 11 editors and an advisory board of over 100 world experts. The official XML Specification, the document defining the rules of XML grammar, is edited by Tim Bray at Textuality and Netscape, Jean Paoli at Microsoft, and C. M. Sperberg-McQueen at the University of Illinois in Chicago. The XML Specification is approved and hosted by the World Wide Web Consortium (W3C) XML Working Group.

What does *Extensible Markup Language* really mean? The term *markup language* in this title is a little misleading, in that a regular markup language defines a way to describe information in a certain class of documents, and this definition is usually unchangeable once designed. But XML is not a fixed markup language that has already been designed and put to use; nor is it a complete document architecture in and of itself. Rather, XML is a markup-design language — or a *metalanguage* — from which markup languages can be derived. After you become familiar with XML, you can define your own customized markup languages for many classes of documents.

The term *extensible* means that you can design as many features of a markup language as you want — providing that you follow the rules of XML, of course. And after you design a markup language, you can keep adding features to it, or extending it.

Compared to Hypertext Markup Language (HTML), which is a standard markup language, XML may be a tricky concept to grasp, but its robustness and flexibility more than make up for its initially intimidating appearance.

XML offers a number of important advantages:

✦ **XML is a powerful alternative to HTML.** Although HTML is an extremely popular and successful markup language, it's limited in a number of ways. For Web developers who have hit a wall with using HTML, XML provides the opportunity to develop new types of markup and document instructions — and entire systems for publishing and document production.

✦ **XML is directly related to SGML.** XML is based on Standard Generalized Markup Language (SGML), the international standard metalanguage for markup languages, and so XML is a simplified form — or a subset — of SGML. XML is as robust as SGML is for purposes of Web development — yet it's considerably easier to learn and implement. XML enables you to serve, receive, and process generic SGML on the Web as you currently can with HTML. XML is fully interoperable with both SGML and HTML, which makes it easier for people with SGML or HTML experience to learn and implement.

✦ **XML is optimized for use on the Internet.** XML was specifically designed with the Web in mind. Since network (both Internet and intranet) connections consume bandwidth and computer-processing resources, XML was designed to reduce the number of document components to be delivered and received. In addition, XML uses standard Web addressing schemes.

✦ **XML is a general-purpose tool.** You can do a lot with XML. Its design supports document authoring, indexing, formatting for database querying, structured machine-to-machine data interchange, and other types of useful applications.

✦ **XML is precise.** Although XML is powerful and versatile, its specification includes a precise and rigorous set of rules for designing markup languages and usable documents. The software that you use to create and view XML documents must strictly conform to the specification's guide on error and exception handling, which means you and other XML users can't get away with sloppy and ambiguous coding. This precision in design makes problems with network and data applications easier to troubleshoot.

✦ **XML belongs to everyone.** XML is an open-systems, platform-independent, nonproprietary, freely available standard. Volunteers from several organizations developed it, and the World Wide Web Consortium currently oversees it. This means that the future of XML probably remains in the hands of the public and not in a single for-profit organization. Developers are excited to invest time in XML because its evolution is likely to provide as many development options as possible while remaining logical and true to the open-systems philosophy.

✦ **XML is a team player.** It provides a natural complement to other computing standards and common programming languages like the Web, Java, and Perl.

✦ **XML is multicultural.** XML was designed to be an international standard, allowing people all over the world to design

XML-based markup languages and document systems in their own languages. XML uses the widely accepted Unicode (ISO 10646) standard for internationalized character sets.

Recently, some organizations and individuals have developed XML applications, or *document type definitions* (DTDs), to standardize document systems for certain fields or industries, such as Chemical Markup Language (CML) and Mathematical Markup Language (MathML).

The popularity and wide-reaching interest in XML only seems to be expanding. A number of Web and network applications are now or soon-to-be XML-compliant, and managers of corporate and government publishing systems are turning to XML for enterprise solutions.

Check out Chapters 2 and 3 of *XML For Dummies* for more about SGML and HTML. For more information about SGML and HTML in this book, *see also* Part VI. You can also find more information on SGML and HTML in the section called "XML, SGML, and HTML" later in this part.

An excellent source of general information about XML is the XML FAQ, or Frequently Asked Questions list, at `www.ucc.ie/xml/`.

Applications for XML

A specification for a new language is useless without a way to implement it. It's good to know that a number of applications for XML are already available and many more are on the horizon.

First, it's important to preempt any confusion you may have about the term *application*. This term is used in XML in two distinct ways:

✦ It's the piece of software that allows you to use and view XML documents. Applications generally involve an XML processor or parser, which allows you to manipulate and generate documents.

✦ It's a markup language derived from XML. For example, Chemical Markup Language (CML) and Mathematical Markup Language (MathML) are both XML applications.

In this book, the term *application* refers to the first point above; an XML application is software that runs XML.

You can find more information on implementing XML in DTDs and documents in Chapter 5 of *XML For Dummies,* as well as in "DTDs and Document Composition" later in this part. You can also find detailed information about various types of XML applications and the components of applications in "Tools and Software" later in this part.

DTDs and Document Composition

Unless you have some time on your hands, you're probably not going to want to study XML for the sake of studying something new. The meat-and-potatoes part of XML — and the exciting and fun part — is creating documents that anyone can read over the Web or an intranet. You can customize your documents to your own specific needs; in fact, an important advantage of XML is being able to set up a standard process of customizing your documents — and set up entire systems of document production. In this way, XML allows you to create both instructions for documents and the documents themselves.

The instructions for documents are contained in a document type definition (DTD). With the help of this book, you can compose your own DTD, use an existing DTD, or modify an existing DTD.

Here's an example of a relatively simple XML document:

```
<?XML version="1.0" encoding="UTF-8"?>
<!DOCTYPE DOC [
    <!ELEMENT DOC (SUBJECT, DATE, AUTHOR, IMG,
    CONTENT)>
    <!ELEMENT SUBJECT (#PCDATA)>
    <!ELEMENT DATE (#PCDATA)>
    <!ELEMENT AUTHOR (#PCDATA)>
    <!ELEMENT IMG EMPTY>
    <!ATTLIST IMG
        SRC ENTITY #REQUIRED
        ALT CDATA #IMPLIED
        ALIGN (LEFT | CENTER | RIGHT) "LEFT">
    <!ELEMENT CONTENT (P+)>
    <!ELEMENT P (#PCDATA)>
]>
<DOC>
. . .
</DOC>
```

In this example, the lines of code from the first line through the line containing just]> is the DTD of the document. Because this DTD is contained entirely within the document, it is referred to as an *internal DTD subset*.

You can understand how a DTD works by looking at each component:

✦ The line `<?XML version="1.0" encoding="UTF-8"?>` is the XML declaration. The XML declaration provides the first set of instructions to the XML processor on how the document should be handled. In this example:

• `XML version="1.0"` means that the document is in XML format, conforming to the XML Specification version 1.0.

- encoding="UTF-8" tells the XML processor to use the 8-bit Unicode character encoding scheme when parsing characters.

✦ The next line, <!DOCTYPE DOC [, marks the beginning of the document type declaration. The document type declaration contains the bulk of the instructions for the XML processor, including element declarations, attribute-list declarations, and more.

✦ <!ELEMENT DOC (SUBJECT, DATE, AUTHOR, IMG, CONTENT)> is the element declaration for the root element DOC. This informs the XML processor that the element DOC contains the child elements SUBJECT, DATE, AUTHOR, IMG, CONTENT, and that these elements must appear in this order within the document.

✦ The elements SUBJECT, DATE, and AUTHOR are each declared to consist of regular character data (#PCDATA).

✦ The element IMG is an empty element. It contains an attribute-list declaration for images (<!ATTLIST IMG) with these attributes:

- SRC ENTITY #REQUIRED means that a reference to an image source file is required.

- ALT CDATA #IMPLIED means that the author of the XML document may include some text as alternative data to the image.

- ALIGN (LEFT | CENTER | RIGHT) "LEFT"> offers the author the choice of aligning the image to the left, center, or right of the document space. The default is a left alignment.

✦ The element declaration for CONTENT, <!ELEMENT CONTENT (P+)>, indicates that at least one paragraph element (P) must be present.

✦ In turn, the element declaration for P, <!ELEMENT P (#PCDATA)>, declares that P must only include regular character data.

✦ The final delimiter of the document type definition is the right-square bracket (]).

✦ The final delimiter of the DTD for this document is the right-angle bracket (>).

After you have access to a DTD and understand the instructions provided in it, you're ready to create documents based on that DTD. You can create as many documents as you'd like for the DTD without having to create a new DTD each time — and herein lies the power of XML. When you put your customized system in place, you can quickly and easily create documents that anyone can read, print, and publish to other formats.

XML For Dummies covers the specification in Chapter 4. For more information on the XML Specification in this book, refer to Part II. For more information on characters, character data, DTDs, and document type declarations, refer to Part III. For more information on elements and attributes, refer to Part IV.

Tools and Software

It's a testament to the promise of XML that already dozens of XML tools and software are available and in development, even though the XML Specification hasn't yet been approved by the World Wide Web Consortium. (At press time, the XML Specification version 1.0 is still in the recommendation phase.)

The XML-compliant and XML-specializing tools are composed of a number of different functions, such as:

+ Browsers

+ Developer's API kits

+ Editors

+ Parsers and processors

+ XML plug-ins and filters

+ XML toolkits

+ Multifeatured XML applications

Currently, commercial vendors and individuals are developing a number of XML software tools. Most XML products are free, because they're still very new, and their developers encourage you to use them and try them out.

Here is a list of XML tools currently available:

Product	Manufacturer/Author	Description
Ælfred XML Parser	Microstar	A Java-based XML parser
DAE SDK and DAE Server SDK	Copernican Solutions	An XML processor for building groves from XML documents
DataChannel XML	DataChannel Development Environment (DXDE) and DXP XML Parser	XML Development tool and a validating XML parser

(continued)

Product	Manufacturer/Author	Description
docproc	Sean Russell	An XML and Extensible Style Language (XSL) document processor
IBM XML for Java	IBM	A validating XML processor for Java
Jumbo	Peter Murray-Rust	A Java-based XML browser designed for the Chemical Markup Language (CML)
Lark	Tim Bray	A nonvalidating XML processor
Larval	Tim Bray	A validating XML processor built on the same code base as Lark
LT XML	The Language Technology Group at the University of Edinburgh	An XML developer's toolkit
MSXML	Microsoft	A validating XML parser written in Java
RXP	Richard Tobin	A nonvalidating XML parser written in C
SAX	Microstar	A Simple API for XML
SAXDOM	Microstar	An implementation of the World Wide Web Consortium (W3C) Document Object Model (DOM) API using Simple API for XML (SAX)
SP Parser	James Clark	An object-oriented toolkit for SGML parsing and entity management that includes support for XML
SX	James Clark	An application of SP that converts SGML into normalized XML
TclXML	Steve Ball	A validating XML parser written in Tcl
XML Editing Mode in PSGML	Lennart Staflin (PSGML), David Megginson, Microstar (XML version)	XML patches for PSGML, an SGML mode for Emacs
XML Styler	ArborText	A tool for creating and modifying XSL style sheets
XMLTok	James Clark	An XML parser written in C
xmlwf	James Clark	An XML well-formedness checker that is part of XMLTok

Product	Manufacturer/Author	Description
XP	James Clark	A nonvalidating XML parser written in Java
Xparse	Jeremie Miller	A JavaScript XML Parser
XSLJ	Henry Thompson	An XSL-to-DSSSL (Extensible Style Language to Document Style Semantics and Specification Language) translator

You can find information on all these tools in the "XML/XSL/XLL Software" section of the SGML/XML Web page located at www.sil.org/sgml/xml.html#xmlSoftware. This section is also updated frequently, so new tools are added as they become available.

Browsers

Once you compose an XML document, you probably want to view the finished product. You can view XML documents — either ones you have created yourself or documents produced by others — through a browser. A *browser* is a piece of software that allows you to view an XML document in a graphical form, the way the author intended it to look.

Some browsers are already emerging, but they're quite new and XML browser development is still in its infancy. Since XML is an open standard, the browsers encompass several different platforms and are written in several programming languages. The emergence of new XML browsers will probably continue to follow this trend, and so you won't be locked into using just one type of browser.

In fact, XML experts currently believe that a number of XML browsers will be necessary to use XML in all its capacities. A browser that accurately displays musical notation, for instance, may not be the best browser for viewing complex mathematical equations, medical records, or screenplays.

Right now, some developers are combining the generic parts of XML into general-purpose browser libraries or toolkits. These generic parts of XML include

✦ Parsing

✦ Data tree management

✦ Searching

✦ Formatting

Such libraries or toolkits make it easier to develop consistent XML DTDs, documents, and document classes. You can then combine these XML applications with other languages and technologies, such as Java, Web browsers, and various scripting languages.

Both manufacturers of the two major Web browsers, Netscape and Microsoft, are currently developing XML facilities for their products. Because of the Internet community's huge interest in XML, it's likely that Web browsers will be XML-compatible in the near future.

Developer's API kits

Programmers and developers may be interested in emerging *application program interface* (API) kits for XML. At press time, a few companies that produce SGML conversion and application development engines are all working on XML API kits.

One currently available tool that can be classified as an XML developer's API kit is the LT XML Toolkit, produced by The Language Technology Group. The LT XML Toolkit includes a variety of modules for processing well-formed XML documents, such as tools for

✦ Searching and extracting data

✦ Down-translation, such as in report generation or formatting

✦ Tokenizing and sorting data

Another API is Microstar SAX: The Simple API for XML. SAX is a draft of an event-based interface for XML parsers. You can use it with Java and other object-oriented languages. SAX is designed to be compatible with any SAX-conformant XML parser.

As XML continues to mature, you'll find more developer's API kits emerging, both in commercial markets and in the public domain.

For more information on The Language Technology Group and its LT XML Toolkit, check the www.ltg.ed.ac.uk/software/xml/. For more information on Microstar SAX, check the SAX Home Page at www.microstar.com/XML/SAX/. You can keep up with new developer's API kits in the XML Industry Support section of the SGML/XML Web page at www.sil.org/sgml/xmlSupport.html and in the Developer's API Kit section (Question D.9) of the XML FAQ at www.ucc.ie/xml/#FAQ-API.

Editors

Most people who access XML will probably just use it for viewing documents and data, the same way people currently use Hypertext Markup Language (HTML) for viewing documents on the Web. But you may want to do more with XML than just view documents that already exist: You may want to author documents yourself.

To create an XML document, you must use some type of software, whether or not it was specifically designed for use with XML coding. Here are some of your choices for an XML-authoring environment:

✦ A plain-text editor, in which you write your entire XML DTDs or documents from scratch. As you may guess, this authoring environment is probably the most time-consuming and has the least support concerning graphic tools, error checking, automation, and so on.

✦ An authoring tool designed especially for XML. Such a tool is considered to be an *XML editor*.

✦ A standard word processor that includes an XML filter or plug-in. This may also be considered to be an XML editor.

Some editors help you visualize your DTD by using graphic aids such as data trees to organize elements and entities. Other editors allow you to easily author XML documents by composing text, selecting various options defined by the DTD from a convenient menu, and applying the options to the text. Ideally, a good editor would allow you to both organize your DTD and compose your documents.

When using an editor to compose your documents, pay attention to whether your DTD supports the UTF-8 (8-bit) or the UTF-16 (16-bit) Unicode character encoding scheme. You want to make sure your editor supports the character encoding scheme that you've chosen.

For more information about character encoding schemes, ***see also*** Part III and Part V of this book.

Parsers and processors

To make sure that you've created an accurate XML DTD or document, you must have some way of processing it. You can do this by using XML-processing software.

Three main components comprise XML-processing software:

✦ The XML parser

✦ The XML processor

✦ The XML software application

The *parser* is a software module that parses, or reads the data of, an XML document and checks it for validity or well-formedness.

The job of the processor overlaps that of the parser. The *processor* reads XML documents, provides access to their content and structure, and reports any errors. An XML processor, or XML-compliant software that includes an XML processor, usually has a parser built into it. For this reason, the terms *parser* and *processor* in relation to XML are often used interchangeably.

The XML parser and processor are also integrally connected to the XML application. The *application* is the interface between the XML processor and the user. An application could have an XML processor built into it, which means that all three components of XML-processing software — the parser, the processor, and the application — are often inseparable.

You're not limited to using an all-in-one package. If you use a plain text editor to author XML documents, for instance, you can use a standalone XML parser to check the code for validity.

The XML Specification, the official set of rules of grammar for XML, provides a precise guide for how an XML processor must work — that is, how it must read XML data, check the data for validity or well-formedness, and send the appropriate information to the XML application. By definition, an XML processor must conform to the rules of the XML Specification.

The XML Specification allows XML processors to operate on either of two levels:

✦ A *nonvalidating XML processor* checks XML documents for well-formedness but not for validity. It can ignore information provided in the DTD and process DTD-less documents without a problem. The XML Specification includes a clever loophole, however: All conforming XML processors, including nonvalidating ones, must be able to read a DTD on request and process it correctly.

✦ A *validating XML processor* checks XML documents for validity, which is a set of additional constraints beyond well-formedness. A validating XML processor, therefore, must be able to read a DTD — and it actually requires the presence of a DTD for validation.

Whether you choose to use a validating or a nonvalidating processor depends on your purposes in using XML documents. A validating processor obviously performs a more complete check on your documents, while a nonvalidating processor parses the data and sends it to the application more quickly. The reduced requirements for nonvalidating processors — and the subsequent reduced need for the use of computer system resources — is an important reason why XML is optimal for use over a network.

Chapter 22 of *XML For Dummies* contains detailed information about ten great XML parsers, validators, and development tools.

What Can I Do with XML?

With XML, you can design a wide variety of document types. In fact, members of the XML community have already created a number of interesting and useful document types and sample documents using XML.

At press time, these are some of the XML document types or documents that are available:

- ✦ Religious markup for *The Bible*
- ✦ Markup for Shakespeare plays, including *Hamlet*
- ✦ Chemical Markup Language (CML)
- ✦ Mathematical Markup Language (MathML)
- ✦ Joseph Conrad's *Heart of Darkness*
- ✦ A weather station demo
- ✦ Channel Definition Format (CDF)
- ✦ A number of informational materials on XML

For more information on XML in current use, check the "XML Examples and Non-Examples" section of Robin Cover's SGML/XML Web page at www.sil.org/sgml/xml.html#examples.

You might be wondering about the possibilities of XML for yourself, in your line of work or area of personal interest. Here are a few ideas for possible XML document types and documents:

- ✦ Transcriptions of ancient texts
- ✦ Technical documentation for engineering projects
- ✦ Medical records
- ✦ Musical notation
- ✦ Manuals for computers and electronic appliances
- ✦ Financial records
- ✦ Academic research and publications
- ✦ Studies of linguistics in multiple languages
- ✦ Reference books
- ✦ Screenplays

✦ Record-keeping and databases

✦ Museum catalog records for a variety of disciplines, including

- Anthropology

- Archaeology

- Biology

- Geology

- Fine arts

- Paleontology

✦ Data interchange between applications

✦ Private corporate and government information and archives

Here's an example of a relatively simple XML document:

```
<?XML version="1.0" standalone="yes"?>
<message>
     <head>Important message</head>
     <body>Please report to my office
       immediately.</body>
</message>
```

A more complex document looks like this:

```
<?XML version="1.0" standalone="no" encoding="UTF-
    16"?>
<!DOCTYPE book SYSTEM "book.dtd">
<book>
<author>Fritjof Capra</author>
<title>The Tao of Physics</title>
<!-This is a great book.->
<preface>
. . .
</preface>
<chap>
<chaptitle>Modern Physics: A Path with a
    Heart?<chaptitle>
. . .
</chap>
. . .
</book>
```

(The three dots indicate a section of content too large for this example.)

As you may realize, the possibilities of what you can create with XML are endless. You might not even be able to imagine some of the future applications of XML, because such applications wouldn't have been possible without it. Once you have a working familiarity with XML, you can create these and many other document types, including ones that haven't been thought of yet.

XML, SGML, and HTML

Without hands-on experience with the languages represented by
these acronyms, confusing them is easy. While a technical relationship between Extensible Markup Language (XML), Standard
Generalized Markup Language (SGML), and Hypertext Markup
Language (HTML) exists, they're each quite different from one
another in important ways.

HTML

SGML was used to design HTML, and so HTML is considered an
SGML document type or an SGML application. As a single application of SGML, HTML defines a fixed set of markup that enables you
to describe a general class of documents that are essentially quite
simple. The HTML document type, or definition, provides authors
with options for headings, paragraphs, lists, graphic images,
hypertext links, multimedia, and some scripting.

Of all the document types that SGML has been used to create,
HTML is by far the most popular and widely used. This is because
HTML is the standard language of the World Wide Web, which has
experienced a phenomenal explosion in interest, development,
and use within the last several years.

While Web developers have become extremely proficient and
clever with HTML, they're quickly approaching the limits of what
HTML can do as a single document type. You can't add markup
definitions to it, change it, or revise it. In fact, a few companies
who manufacture HTML-based Web browsers have added their
own features to HTML. Most of the new features haven't been
approved for the public standard of HTML, however, and so each
Web browser has developed its own proprietary version of HTML
as a result. This led to confusion, "browser wars," and lots of
annoyed Web developers. While HTML continues to be an important authoring and document exchange tool, many computer and
network applications being developed now require a more robust
and flexible infrastructure — such as XML.

If you're deciding whether to learn and use XML instead of sticking
with tried-and-true HTML, consider the following advantages of
XML over HTML:

✦ If you're an author or a content provider, you can design your
   own document types using XML. You can customize a document type to a particular audience, community, or industry.

✦ Using XML, you won't have to constantly tweak and fiddle
   with a single document type (such as HTML) to achieve
   the look, feel, and capabilities that you want out of your

documents. Any time you want a new feature, you can add it to a document type. You can design an entire set of features for one document type and another set of features for another document type. You can create and use as many document types as necessary.

✦ You can more easily access and reuse your information, because the precise-yet-flexible markup of XML can be used by any XML-compliant software instead of being restricted to software made by specific manufacturers, as in the case with HTML.

✦ XML supports the structures that you need to represent database *schemas* or object-oriented hierarchies. You can nest document structures to any level of complexity. This makes XML an excellent tool for automated database access and data exchange.

✦ XML supports validation. By design, XML processors and applications must check XML data for structural validity and flag any errors. HTML browsers, by comparison, are flexible — often, too flexible — when reading HTML code, and they tend to forgive inaccurate coding.

✦ Since valid XML documents are technically SGML documents, you can use valid XML documents outside the Web or in an SGML-compliant environment. With HTML, you're mostly restricted to use on the Web. XML therefore provides an excellent bridge for exchanging content in the same format from one computer system to another.

Keep in mind that you don't have to take an either-or approach to XML and HTML. If you already know HTML, you may have an easier time learning XML. In addition, you can use your knowledge of HTML and experience in working with a markup language to define new document types. In fact, if you've ever been working with HTML and wished that you could do something that was impossible, you now have a chance to design the markup language of your dreams with XML. Furthermore, you can easily convert documents conforming to the World Wide Web Consortium HTML 3.2 specification to XML. Knowing both HTML and XML can thus be a very powerful combination.

For more detailed information about HTML and its relationship to XML, check out Chapter 2 of *XML For Dummies.*

For more information on HTML, check the World Wide Web Consortium's HTML Home Page at w3c.org/MarkUp/.

SGML

SGML is an International Organization for Standardization (ISO) specification used for defining markup languages. SGML comes first in the chronology of standard markup languages, and so it's the mother tongue of a wide variety of both proprietary and public document types. Since SGML has been available for over a decade, its base of support includes a plethora of books, articles, software titles, and human expertise.

Although SGML is extremely powerful, it's not something that people decide to study casually. It's complicated, full of obscure options, and somewhat intimidating because of its steep learning curve. It usually takes a while to create a working SGML application, so most computer users rely on ones that already exist, such as HTML.

XML provides an excellent alternative to SGML, because it's a subset of SGML — yet it retains much of the power that SGML has to create any kind of document type. The designers of XML borrowed much of the syntax and many of the concepts from SGML, but left out some of the more cumbersome structures and optional features of SGML. They also made sure that XML is fully interoperable with SGML; that is, any valid XML document is an SGML document and can be used in SGML tools and software.

If you're familiar with SGML, you can pick up XML in no time. If not, don't worry — with a little time and patience, you can learn XML and start creating your own DTDs and documents fairly soon.

For more information about SGML and its differences from XML, check out Chapter 3 of *XML For Dummies*. For more about those differences in this book, ***see also*** Part VI.

You can find a comprehensive guide to SGML and SGML resources, including some XML resources, at Robin Cover's SGML/XML Web page at www.sil.org/sgml/. The section called "XML and/versus SGML" of the SGML/XML Web page, located at www.sil.org/sgml/xml.html#sgml-xml, contains a number of links to articles and documentation about the differences between XML and SGML. You may also find the "World Wide Web Consortium's Comparison of SGML and XML," an extensive document outlining the technical differences between XML and SGML, to be very useful; you can find it at www.w3.org/TR/NOTE-sgml-xml.

XML

XML provides an excellent alternative to both the complexity of SGML and the limitations of HTML. XML is actually an abbreviated version of SGML — one that is optimized for use on the Web. Compared to SGML, XML simplifies

✦ Defining document types

✦ Authoring and managing SGML-defined documents

✦ Transmitting and exchanging documents over the Web

You should remember that XML is essentially SGML, so that valid XML files may still be parsed and validated the same as any other SGML file. By definition, all valid XML documents are SGML documents. It's therefore more accurate to classify XML as SGML than to think of it as HTML++.

You can find more introductory information on XML in "About XML" earlier in this part. Details about XML itself also appear in Chapter 1 of *XML For Dummies*.

Part II

The XML Specification

This part introduces you to the XML Specification, which is the official definition of how you should design XML DTDs and compose documents. The XML Specification itself is long and detailed, and much of it lends little assistance to someone actively using XML. Understanding how the specification works as a whole, however, is key to creating correct DTDs and working documents.

In this part . . .

✔ **Understanding the difference between logical and physical structures**

✔ **Using the standard notation to analyze XML rules**

✔ **Looking at some common syntactic constructs**

✔ **Using literals**

✔ **Designing names and name tokens**

Logical and Physical Structures

How you structure XML documents involves the organization, syntax, and other general rules of XML documents. XML documents have two types of structure:

+ **Logical structure:** This type includes elements, attributes, and the rules and specifications associated with elements.

+ **Physical structure:** This type involves entities, types of characters, and the rules and specifications associated with entities.

Any rule that addresses logical structure as a whole is a *single logical structure;* similarly, rules that apply to the physical structure of one or more documents are *individual physical structures.*

For XML documents to work properly, you must order the logical and physical structures properly.

Logical structures

If you were to take an XML document apart, you would see that it involves two ingredients: materials (made up of text) and the way in which the materials are organized. The way in which the materials are organized is referred to as the *logical structure* of the document. Individual logical structures, therefore, are the technical rules that dictate how the text in XML documents are to be organized.

XML documents are specifically organized by XML components such as declarations, elements, comments, character references, and processing instructions. The method by which these components work is markup within XML documents. Examples of logical structures include

+ Definition of symbols.

+ Logical order of items within an expression.

+ Number of occurrences for each item.

+ Other relevant instructions.

In particular, logical structures involve *elements,* which are small pieces of instructions that you either delimit by start-tags and end-tags or specify as an empty-element tag. Each XML document must contain at least one element.

Each element has a type, which is identified by name — or the element's *generic identifier* (GI). Elements often have a set of attribute specifications, but not always. Of the elements that have attribute specifications, each attribute specification must have a name and a value.

This rule of the XML Specification provides a very generic example of an element:

```
element ::= EmptyElemTag | STag content ETag [ wfc:
    Element Type Match ]
```

In this logical structure, `element` offers a choice of using either `EmptyElemTag`, an empty element tag, or `STag content ETag`, which indicates content text sandwiched between a start-tag preceding the content and an end-tag following it. The `wfc:` code refers to a *Well-Formedness Constraint*. In this case, the `Element Type Match` constraint indicates that the name of an element's end-tag must match the element type in the start-tag.

Here's how a well-formed pair of matching element tags could appear in a document:

```
<tag>content</tag>
```

Notice that the element type `tag` matches on both sides of `content`; the end-tag is marked by the slash (/) at the beginning of the element type name.

To understand how the notation of this code works, ***see also*** "Notation in XML Rules" in this part. For more information on logical structures, elements, and attributes, ***see also*** Part IV. For more information on well-formed XML documents, ***see also*** Part III. Chapters 5 and 6 of *XML For Dummies* contain extensive discussions of XML structure and markup notation.

Beyond using the correct syntax, you may use any element type or attribute you wish, with the exception of names that begin with `XML` itself, including any combination of uppercase and lowercase letters of `XML`, such as `xml`, `Xml`, or `xMl`. Names beginning with anything that matches `(('X'|'x')('M'|'m')('L'|'l'))` are reserved for standardization in the current or future World Wide Web Consortium XML specification.

Physical structures

Physical structures involve *entities,* which are virtual storage units found in XML documents. These virtual storage units contain content — or text found between start-tags and end-tags — and are identified by name. A few examples of physical structures include

- ✦ Allowed character sets.
- ✦ Constraints for document well-formedness and validity.
- ✦ Rules for character encoding.
- ✦ The textual content of a document.

For examples of these physical structures and more information about physical structures in general, ***see also*** Part V.

Each XML document must have at least one entity. If a document contains only one entity, it must be the document entity, which serves as the starting point for the XML processor. The document entity may include the entire document. Entities need not be identified by name; you can identify them through a public identifier stored externally.

For more information about public identifiers, ***see also*** Part III.

Entities may be either *parsed* or *unparsed*.

+ **Parsed:** A parsed entity's contents contain text that is an integral part of the document. This *replacement text* replaces the name of the parsed entity. You invoke parsed entities by name using entity references.

+ **Unparsed:** If you need to use content that involves both text and nontext, or text that is not XML, you should use an unparsed entity. Like a parsed entity, you do identify an unparsed entity by name. Unlike a parsed entity, though, an unparsed entity has an associated notation for a file format rather than replacement text. You can set any content to unparsed entities, except for the name of a notation and associated identifiers required by the XML processor. You invoke unparsed entities by a name that you provide in the value of ENTITY or ENTITIES attributes.

Here are two types of parsed entities:

+ **General entities:** Used within the document content.

+ **Parameter entities:** Used within the DTD.

General entities and parameter entities each use a different syntax and are recognized in different contexts.

To find details of entities and entity processing, ***see also*** Part V.

Notation in XML Rules

XML rules — each complete line of the XML Specification — indicate instructions for DTDs and documents. XML rules make up the grammar of XML; essentially, they define the legal syntax and sets of allowed codes or sequences of characters for DTDs and documents, as well as describe instructions for XML processors and applications.

In order for XML documents to be well-formed or valid, DTDs and documents must follow these rules of grammar. The syntax of the rules themselves is referred to as *notation*.

The syntax of these rules is referred to as *notation*. Don't confuse my use of the word *notation* in this section with the term *notation* as used in discussions on unparsed entities and notation declarations.

Here is the form of a standard rule of XML grammar:

```
symbol ::= expression
```

This notation contains the following parts:

+ `symbol` refers to the name given to a particular rule.

+ `::=` is the delimiter, which separates the symbol from the expression.

+ `expression` refers to the definition of the symbol, or what the symbol is instructed to do. An expression is treated as a unit, and it may carry the % prefix operator or one of the suffix operators: ?, *, or +.

A sample notation looks like this:

```
PCData ::= [^<&]*
```

The notation breaks down like this:

+ `PCData` is the symbol for character data.

+ `::=` is the delimiter, which separates the symbol from the expression.

+ `[^<&]*` is the expression. The square brackets (`[ ]`) indicate that the characters inside are part of a set — a set that must be examined first and then operated on by a suffix operator, if one is present.

This notation indicates a rule for character data.

Chapter 9 of *XML For Dummies* contains several tables of special characters that you can use in your markup. For more information about character data in this book, ***see also*** Part III.

Expression code syntax and meaning

The expression (the part of a rule on the right-hand side of the `::=`) contains one or more specific codes. Each code provides an important piece of information in determining the instructions and definition assigned to the symbol. The following table shows the syntax of expression codes and the meaning of each one.

Expression Code	Meaning
#xN	An expression that matches a character in the Unicode character set. The number of leading zeros in #xN is insignificant; N is a hexadecimal integer.
[a-zA-Z], [#xN-#xN]	Represents any character with a value in the range(s) indicated. This range includes every consecutive item within that range.
[^a-z], [^#xN-#xN]	The ^ means *not*. This code represents any character with a value outside the indicated range.
[^abc], [^#xN#xN#xN]	Represents any character with a value not among the characters given.
"string"	Represents a literal string matching that given inside the double quotes.
'string'	Represents a literal string matching that given inside the single quotes (called *apostrophes* in programming, even though technically only the closing single quote is an apostrophe).
a b	*a* followed by *b*.
a | b	*a* or *b* but not both. (One item from the list at most.)
a - b	The set of strings represented by *a* but not represented by *b*.

Expression extensions

The following codes that you find in the notation of the XML Specification are used to append information or instructions to expressions.

Expression Extensions	Meaning
/* . . . */	A comment. (For insight into how rules work within the XML Specification, read the comments written by the developers of the XML Specification. You can find useful comments next to rules throughout the specification.)
[WFC: . . .]	Well-formedness check, identified by name.
[VC: . . .]	Validity check, identified by name.

Here is an example of a rule that contains a comment:

```
PCData ::= [^<&]* /* Typical rule for character
    data */
```

For a breakdown and explanation of this rule for character data, *see also* the "Notation in XML Rules" section in this part and the example in the "Suffix operators" section.

The text within the /* . . . */ code is a comment, which is not technically part of the rule; the comment was included by the XML Specification authors to help you understand how the rule works.

The following example of a rule contains both validity and well-formedness checks:

```
Attribute ::= Name Eq AttValue [ VC: Attribute
    Value Type ]
[ WFC: No External Entity References ]
```

The expression, or right-hand side of the ::= delimiter, is as follows:

✦ In the expression, the VC: within square brackets ([ ]) means "validity check" or "validity constraint." This particular validity constraint refers to the Attribute Value Type, which means that you must have declared the attribute; the value must be of the type declared for it. (For more information about attributes, *see also* Part IV.)

✦ In the next line of the expression, the WFC: within square brackets ([ ]) means "well-formedness check" or "well-formedness constraint." This particular well-formedness constraint refers to No External Entity References. This constraint means that attribute values can't contain entity references to external entities.

Check out Chapter 5 of *XML For Dummies* to get the details on validity and well-formedness in XML markup. For more information about validity and well-formedness checks in this book, *see also* Part III. For more information about entities, *see also* Part V.

Prefix operator

If you have an expression unit a, the prefix operator (%) specifies that in the external DTD subset a parameter entity may occur in the text at the position where a may occur.

The prefix operator % has lower precedence than any of the suffix operators ?, *, or +; so %a* and %(a*) mean the same thing. The result of including a parameter entity reference at the indicated location must match a*.

For more information about parameter entities, *see also* Part V.

Suffix operators

Expression codes may be accompanied by suffix operators: the question mark (?), the plus sign (+), and the asterisk (*).

The following table explains each suffix operator as it applies to the expression code a:

Suffix Operator	Meaning
a?	*a* or nothing; *a* is optional.
a+	One or more occurrences of *a*.
a*	Zero or more occurrences of *a*.

In this notation:

PCData ::= [^<&]*

The expression, or right-hand side of the ::= delimiter, is as follows:

+ In the expression [^<&]*, the square brackets ([ ]) must be examined first and then operated on by the suffix operator *.

+ Inside the square brackets, the ^ indicates "not any of the following characters or range of characters." Because only two characters follow the ^, < and &, and no dash is present to indicate a range of characters, the notation ^<& means "neither the less-than nor the ampersand character may be used."

+ The * means that there can be any number of occurrences of the previously defined character set.

Putting it all together, [^<&]* means that there can be any number (including zero) of characters other than < and & present.

Syntactic Constructs

Some of the symbols that you find in XML grammar follow a specific syntax, which is referred to as a *syntactic construct.* Some common syntactic constructs include literals, names, and tokens.

In an XML rule, the expression may include letters, digits, or other characters. The full sets of letters, digits, and other characters belong to character classes. Each character within a character class is denoted by a hexadecimal code. (***See also*** Part V for a detailed table of character classes.)

White space is an example of a common syntactic construct using characters in the expression.

```
S ::= (#x20 | #x9 | #xD | #xA)+
```

This rule indicates that S, the symbol for white space, may consist of one or more of the four choices listed in the expression. Each of these four choices in the expression is a code from the standard Unicode character database:

+ The first code, #x20, denotes a space character.

+ The second code, #x9, denotes a carriage return.

+ The third code, #xD, denotes a line feed.

+ The fourth code, #xA, denotes a tab.

So, according to this syntactic construct, white space is made up of one or more space characters, carriage returns, line feeds, or tabs.

To understand how the notation of this code works, *see also* "Notation in XML Rules" earlier in this chapter.

Literals

If you need to define an exact string of characters to use in a document, or if you need to define a set of characters that must not be used, you may do this by specifying literal data. Literal data, or a set of literals, is any character string inside quotes — but the quotation marks themselves that are used as delimiters for the string aren't part of the character string defined by the literal.

You use literals to specify content in

+ Internal entities.

+ Attribute values.

+ External identifiers.

One rule specifying an internal entity is:

```
EntityValue ::= '"' ([^%&"] | PEReference
    | Reference)* ' | "'" ([^%&'] | PEReference
    | Reference)* "'"
```

This rule may initially seem complex, but it can easily be broken down.

+ The symbol, EntityValue, denotes that this rule applies to an internal entity.

✦ What follows the : : = delimiter is the expression, or definition, of the internal entity. The entire expression is `'"'` `([^%&"]` `| PEReference | Reference)*` `'` `|` `"'"` `([^%&']` `|` `PEReference | Reference)*` `"'"`.

✦ This expression can be broken down into two parts: `'"'` `([^%&"]` `| PEReference | Reference)*` `'` and `"'"` `([^%&']` `| PEReference | Reference)*` `"'"`, divided by the logical "or" (`|`).

✦ Each of the two main parts of the expression can be broken down further. The first part, `'"'` `([^%&"]` `| PEReference | Reference)*` `'`, indicates that a choice exists between the character set excluding the percent sign, ampersand, and quotation mark; the parameter-entity reference; and the entity reference. This part is proceeded by an asterisk, indicating that zero or more occurrences of this definition can occur.

✦ Similarly, the second part, `"'"` `([^%&']` `| PEReference | Reference)*` `"'"`, indicates that a choice exists between the character set excluding the percent sign, ampersand, and apostrophe; the parameter-entity reference; and the entity reference. This part is also proceeded by an asterisk, indicating that zero or more occurrences of this definition can occur.

Putting it all together, this means that the internal entity is defined by zero or more occurrences of any character but %, &, or either the quotation mark or the apostrophe, depending on which of the two parts is relevant; or a parameter-entity reference; or an entity reference.

You may have noticed that if the definition involves a quotation mark, the delimiter used as a boundary around the definition is an apostrophe. Conversely, if the definition involves an apostrophe, the delimiter used as a boundary around the definition is a quotation mark. This difference in delimiters is because if a quotation mark is in the definition, then the delimiter must be a quotation mark that is itself surrounded by apostrophes, and vice versa for an apostrophe in the definition. This is why so much space is required to indicate something relatively simple. Be sure that you keep this rule in mind to avoid confusion and problems later on.

Here is a similar rule that specifies the value of an attribute:

```
AttValue ::= '"' ([^<&"] | Reference)* '"' | "'"
    ([^<&'] | Reference)* "'"
```

The way this rule works is very similar to how the internal entity works in the prior example. Two differences exist between these two examples. First, the attribute value excludes the less-than sign

(<) instead of the percent sign. Also, no parameter-entity references are present in the expression as there are in the expression of the internal entity.

To make sure that no quotation marks or apostrophes are used in external identifiers, the literal data is defined by these two rules:

```
SystemLiteral ::= SkipLit
SkipLit ::= ('"' [^"]* '"') | ("'" [^']* "'")
```

The two rules are used in conjunction and can be analyzed together.

✦ SystemLiteral, or the literal data for the external identifier, is defined as SkipLit.

✦ SkipLit is merely a pointer to another set of instructions — basically, a rule whose expression says ('"' [^"]* '"') | ("'" [^']* "'").

✦ Breaking down ('"' [^"]* '"') | ("'" [^']* "'"), you can see that SkipLit indicates that either ('"' [^"]* '"') or ("'" [^']* "'") must be observed.

• The first set within the expression of SkipLit, ('"' [^"]* '"'), indicates that zero or more occurrences of the quotation mark may not be used.

• Similarly, the latter set, ("'" [^']* "'"), indicates that zero or more occurrences of the apostrophe may not be used. (Note that when referring to quotation marks in literal data, quotes inside apostrophes are used to delimit the literal; conversely, apostrophes inside quotes are used to delimit the literal containing an apostrophe.)

✦ Putting together the entire SkipLit expression means that any number of occurrences of quotation marks or apostrophes may be used.

✦ The expression of SkipLit is then applied to SystemLiteral.

✦ Because SkipLit is basically a generic rule for a literal that excludes quotes and apostrophes, it can be applied elsewhere. It basically means that the entire literal can be skipped without scanning for markup within it.

Another purpose of literals in an external identifier is to specify the characters that may or may not be used in a Public ID. Take the following two rules:

```
PubidLiteral ::= '"' PubidChar* '"' | "'"
    (PubidChar - "'")* "'"
PubidChar ::= #x20 | #xD | #xA | [a-zA-Z0-9] | [-
    '()+,./:=?;!*#@$_%]
```

In a similar way to the prior `SystemLiteral` example, these two
rules are used in conjunction and can be analyzed together.

✦ `PubidLiteral`, or the literal data for the Public ID, is defined
as `'"' PubidChar* '"' | "'" (PubidChar - "'")*
"'"`.

✦ You'll notice that parts of the expression for `PubidLiteral`
refer to a rule for `PubidChar`, or literal data for the characters
used in the Public ID.

✦ In order to understand what the expression for `PubidChar`,
`#x20 | #xD | #xA | [a-zA-Z0-9] | [-'()+,./:=?]`,
means, break down and identify each piece of code.

✦ The logical "or" (`|`) separates `#x20`, `#xD`, `#xA`, `[a-zA-Z0-9]`,
and `[-'()+,./:=?;!*#@$_%]`.

✦ The first three items are codes from the standard Unicode
character database: `#x20` denotes a space character, `#xD`
denotes a line feed, and `#xA` denotes a tab.

✦ The next item is a set of characters: `[a-zA-Z0-9]`. This
denotes the range from a through z of both lowercase letters
and uppercase letters, as well as the range of digits from zero
through nine.

✦ The last item is another set of characters: `[-'()+,./
:=?;!*#@$_%]`. This time the set represents individual
characters (a hyphen, apostrophe, parentheses, plus sign, and
so forth) rather than a range.

✦ Substitute the definition of `PubidChar` into the expression
for `PubidLiteral`: `'"' PubidChar* '"' | "'"
(PubidChar - "'")* "'"`. Because `PubidChar` represents
this choice of characters, `PubidLiteral` allows a choice
between a literal string of zero or more `PubidChar` characters, or zero or more `PubidChar` characters without an
apostrophe.

Here is a document type declaration that contains a public
identifier:

```
<!DOCTYPE Dummies PUBLIC "-//DUMMIES//DTD Dummies
  1.0 document//EN">
```

Note that within the quotes, the public identifier can contain a
variety of characters, including white-space characters.

For more information about public identifiers, document type
declarations, and white space, **see also** Part III.

Names and tokens

In XML, the labels representing distinctive units of information within rules are *tokens*. A *name* is a token that begins with a letter, an underscore, or a colon. After the first character, other letters, underscores, or colons, as well as digits, periods, or standard Unicode combining characters or extenders can exist. The characters that follow the initial character may appear in any combination.

This XML rule describes the composition of a Name:

```
Name ::= (Letter | '_' | ':') (NameChar)*
```

Analyzing the expression of this rule is simple:

+ `(Letter | '_' | ':') (NameChar)*` can be divided into two parts. `(NameChar)*` must follow `(Letter | '_' | ':')`.

+ The first part, `(Letter | '_' | ':')`, indicates that only one of the following can begin a Name: a letter, an underscore, or a colon.

+ The second part, `(NameChar)*`, indicates that NameChar can occur zero or more times after the first character.

But how do you know what `NameChar` is or does? In order for the rule described above to work properly, it exists in conjunction with the `NameChar` rule:

```
NameChar ::= Letter | Digit | '.' | '-' | '_' | ':'
           | CombiningChar | Extender
```

The expression of `NameChar` indicates that you have a choice between using a letter, digit, period, hyphen, underscore, colon, or standard Unicode combining character or extender. Because the `Name` rule includes a reference to `NameChar`, the `NameChar` rule thus completes the `Name` definition.

Take this one step further, and you can have multiple Names. A multiple version of `Name`, or `Names`, can be composed of a single Name or a Name followed by a series of white spaces and Names. This rule defines `Names`:

```
Names ::= Name (S Name)*
```

If you have three individual `Names`: Joe, Bob, and Sally, an example of Names that includes only one Name is:

```
Joe
```

An example of Names that includes more than one Name is:

```
Joe Sally
```

or:

```
Joe Bob Sally
```

or:

```
Joe Joe Sally Bob Joe Sally
```

Although the colon character is explicitly included within rules pertaining to Names, and XML processors should accept the colon as a name character, it is reserved for experimental purposes within the XML standards community. It is best at this time to avoid using the colon in name definitions.

Just like a Name, a name token is made up of any mixture of name characters. In rules, name tokens are abbreviated as Nmtoken.

Nmtoken rules are very similar to Name rules:

```
Nmtoken  ::= (NameChar)+
Nmtokens ::= Nmtoken (S Nmtoken)*
```

The major difference is that the set of characters that can make up a name token is less restrictive than the set of characters for Names; name tokens can start with any name character, not just a letter or an underscore.

As long as the syntax is correct, you may use any Name or name token that you wish, except for ones that begin with XML itself. This includes any combination of uppercase and lowercase letters of XML, such as xml, Xml, or xMl. Names beginning with anything that matches (('X' | 'x')('M' | 'm')('L' | 'l')) are reserved for standardization in the current or future World Wide Web Consortium XML Specification.

Part III

Designing an XML DTD

If the flesh of XML is the document, then the heart and soul of XML is the description of how the document works: the markup it uses, the content of the data, the external files it references, and specific instructions for the XML processor. You find this description in the document type definition (DTD) associated with the document. To get the most use out of XML, you should know how to create and use DTDs as efficiently as possible. A DTD is like a toolbox full of tools; this chapter explains these tools.

In this part . . .

✔ Using appropriate characters and character data

✔ Designing markup, using CDATA sections, and processing instructions

✔ Including comments

✔ Dissecting the parts of a DTD

✔ Deciding whether to use an internal or an external DTD subset, or both

✔ Learning the difference between well-formed and valid documents

✔ Understanding how white space works

Characters

The smallest and most basic unit of an XML document is a *character*. Specifically, characters make up parsed data, which, in addition to unparsed data, makes up *entities*.

For more information about entities and parsed data, **see also** Part V.

Character data

The characters in parsed data serve two purposes: to make up the textual content of an XML document and to form the XML markup applied to and surrounding the content. The characters that make up the content are called *character data*.

As a whole, characters in parsed data is called *text*, which is a meaningful set of one or more characters; essentially, a sequence of characters. Therefore, text makes up both content and markup. If a section of text is not markup, it must be character data.

The character data and markup that make up text don't need to be presented in any specific order, other than following logical and syntactic constraints. The character data and markup are usually mixed together throughout the text of a document; predictably, a mixture of character data and markup is called *mixed content*.

A small section of mixed content could look like this:

```
<p>You will need to look at <part>Part IV</part>
    and <part>Part V</part> for more information.
    </p>
```

Note that this section of content contains both regular text and markup; mixed content is simply a mixture of the two.

In terms of computer processing, a character is a chunk of data that organizes, controls, or represents information. XML characters are based on the standard *ISO 10646 character encoding scheme*, or *Unicode*. Unicode supports encoding schemes of 8-bit character sets, 16-bit sets, and even 32-bit sets. Any alphabetic letter, digit, or special byte-code within the Unicode character set is a character.

See also Part V for detailed descriptions of the character set. *XML For Dummies* Chapter 9 contains a great deal of information regarding special characters. For more information about the Unicode character set, check out the Unicode Consortium home page at www.unicode.org/.

You find these few examples of characters throughout XML documents:

- ✦ The English alphabetic set A through Z, both uppercase and lowercase—as well as alphabetic sets of many other languages.
- ✦ Arabic digits 0 through 9
- ✦ The less-than character: <
- ✦ The greater-than character: >
- ✦ The question mark: ?
- ✦ The exclamation point: !
- ✦ The quotation mark: "
- ✦ The apostrophe: '
- ✦ The percent sign: %
- ✦ A tab
- ✦ A carriage return
- ✦ A line feed

This list is not complete; other characters are pertinent and often necessary to XML use.

Regarding the content of elements: Character data is any string of characters that does not contain the start-delimiter of any markup.

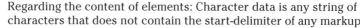

For example, if an element for a first name is defined in a DTD:

```
<!ELEMENT firstname (#PCDATA)>
```

and a corresponding XML document contains this string:

```
<firstname>Mariva</firstname>
```

then the only character data in the element content are the letters M,a,r,i,v, and a, respectively.

See also Part IV for detailed information about elements. Check out the "Markup Design" section later in this part for more information on markup, or check out Chapter 6 of *XML For Dummies* to get the markup big picture.

Similarly, in a CDATA section, character data consists of any string of characters that does not include the CDATA-section-close delimiter,]]>.

For more information, ***see also*** "CDATA sections" within "Markup Design" later in this part.

Special characters

XML reserves several characters for use in certain circumstances:

✦ Ampersand: &

✦ Less-than sign (sometimes referred to as the left-angle bracket): <

✦ Greater-than sign (sometimes referred to as the right-angle bracket): >

✦ Apostrophe (sometimes referred to as the single quote): '

✦ Quotation mark (sometimes referred to as the double quote): "

When these characters represent themselves, they appear in their literal form. The only circumstances in which the ampersand (&) and the less-than sign (<) may appear in their literal form include

✦ When serving as markup delimiters.

✦ Within a comment.

✦ Within a processing instruction.

✦ Within a CDATA section.

✦ Within the literal entity value of an internal entity declaration.

For more information about internal entities and entity declarations, *see also* Part V. You can find more information on CDATA sections in the section called "Markup Design" later in this part.

To use these special characters elsewhere, such as in the actual content of your document, you must use their equivalent escape sequences. These escape sequences are either the corresponding Unicode hexadecimal codes or special escape-character strings.

Basic Latin Character	*Unicode Hexadecimal Assignment (with Delimiters)*	*Escape-Character String*
&	&#x26;	&amp;
<	&#x3C;	&lt;
>	&#x3E;	&gt;
'	&#x27;	&apos;
"	&#x22;	&quot;

If you use the greater-than sign (>) in conjunction with the string]]> in document content, you must use the > escape-character sequence for the XML processor to avoid confusion.

An interesting way to remember that you can't use the ampersand (&) literally in content is knowing that the ampersand character is the delimiter that marks the beginning of an escape-character sequence. If you were to display & in an XML document, the code would appear as &amp;.

The rule in the XML Specification that defines character data uses the symbol `CharData`:

```
CharData ::= [^<&]* - ([^<&]* ']]>' [^<&]*)
```

This is the one-line technical equation for the directive described above. I explain CDATA sections in the "Markup Design" section later in this part.

Specification

Like any other directive in XML, the set of characters, or *character range,* is defined by a rule of grammar in the XML Specification.

The rule that addresses the character range is

```
Char ::= #x9 | #xA | #xD | [#x20-#D7FF] | [#xE000-
    #xFFFD] | [#x10000-#x10FFFF]
/* any Unicode character, excluding the surrogate
    blocks, FFFE, and FFFF. */
```

Following standard XML Specification notation, you can break down this rule to find out the specific codes comprising the character range:

✦ First, note that the symbol for character is `Char`. If `Char` appears as part of an expression in any other rule, then you must apply its definition (the character range) to the appropriate place in that rule.

✦ Take the first part of the expression, `#x9 | #xA | #xD | [#x20-#D7FF] | [#xE000-#xFFFD] | [#x10000-#x10FFFF]`, and divide each unit by the logical "or" (|): `#x9`, `#xA`, `#xD`, `[#x20-#D7FF]`, `[#xE000-#xFFFD]`, and `[#x10000-#x10FFFF]`. To translate the items in the expression, you need to know the following hexadecimal values assigned to Unicode characters:

✦ The first code, `#x9`, denotes a carriage return.

✦ The second code, `#xA`, denotes a tab.

✦ The third code, `#xD`, denotes a line feed.

✦ The fourth unit is a range, starting with `#x20`, which denotes a space character. The range extends far into the Unicode character set. (Parts of this Unicode block, or set of characters, have not been mapped yet and are beyond the scope of this book.)

◆ Two other blocks of Unicode are part of the XML character range: [#xE000-#xFFFD] and [#x10000-#x10FFFF].

◆ The comment /* any Unicode character, excluding the surrogate blocks, FFFE, and FFFF. */ explains that the character range basically includes any Unicode character, except for the small block of codes #xFFFE through #xFFFF.

Putting it all together, a character that is legal in XML, or Char, is defined as one of the preceding choices of the Unicode set.

The character range is huge and can accommodate you in creating any type of XML DTD or document.

DTD Design for Effectiveness

Since the terms *document type declaration* and *document type definition (DTD)* are so similar, some XML users and authorities use them interchangeably. You should keep in mind, however, an important distinction between the two, and knowing this distinction helps you use XML more effectively.

The difference: The XML document type declaration contains and/or references a set of markup declarations that provide the grammar for a single document or an entire class of documents. The document type definition, or DTD, is the set of grammar found in or referenced by document type declaration.

Specifically, the document type declaration does one or both of these two things:

◆ It points to an *external DTD subset* that contains markup declarations. This external subset is another file that the XML processor can read along with the XML document file to process the document. Because the external subset is a separate file referenced by the document type declaration within the document, it is a special type of external entity.

◆ It contains the markup declarations directly, or *locally,* in the prolog of the document. This set of markup declarations in the prolog is the *internal DTD subset*. The internal DTD subset is sometimes known as the *local* DTD. The internal subset may contain a pointer to the external subset.

For more information about external entities, ***see also*** "Declaring Entities" in Part V.

You need to remember the following about the DTD for an XML document: It consists of both subsets, external and internal, taken together. The DTD contains all of this information as a whole.

Specifically, the information within the DTD may include

✦ The allowed element types.

✦ The characteristics of each element type, such as allowed attributes and content.

✦ Allowed notations.

✦ Allowed entities.

✦ References to external entities.

✦ Comments providing internal documentation.

The syntax for the reference to an external subset within a document's document type declaration looks like this:

```
<!DOCTYPE rootElementName SYSTEM
    "filename.dtd">
```

In the document type declaration, the *system identifier* filename.dtd provides the *uniform resource identifier (URI)*, which is the filename and necessary path or URL, immediately following SYSTEM.

If you reference a public external DTD subset, you use a *public identifier* like this:

```
<!DOCTYPE rootElementName PUBLIC
    "URL" SYSTEM "URL">
```

Both the system identifier and the public identifier are known as *external identifiers*.

At press time, the World Wide Web Consortium is still developing the URI. You can find more information about it at www.w3.org/Addressing/.

Here is an example of an XML document with a document type declaration that contains a reference to an external subset but doesn't contain an internal subset:

```
<?xml version="1.0"?>
<!DOCTYPE form SYSTEM "form.dtd">
<form>The content of the form is
    located here.</form>
```

The system identifier form.dtd is the URI of the external DTD subset for this document. You can find all necessary markup declarations for this document in the external subset form.dtd.

A document containing a brief but complete internal DTD subset without a reference to an external DTD subset looks like this:

```
<?xml version="1.0"?>
<!DOCTYPE form [
<!ELEMENT form (#PCDATA)>
]>
<form> The content of the form is
    located here.</form>
```

Notice that this document provides all the necessary declarations locally, within its own document type declaration.

Finally, here is a document that contains both an internal DTD subset and a pointer to an external DTD subset:

```
<?xml version="1.0"?>
<!DOCTYPE form SYSTEM
    "genericform.dtd" [
<!ELEMENT form (#PCDATA)>
]>
<form> The content of the form is
    located here.</form>
```

Remember, the DTD is the information from both subsets — the local declarations and the system file `genericform.dtd` — combined.

External DTD subsets: When to use

Why would you reference an external DTD subset when you can include all the necessary grammar information locally? Here are a few reasons to use and reference an external DTD subset:

✦ If you need to produce an entire *class* of documents — that is, a group of documents that conform to the same rules of grammar — you can tightly control that class by using a single DTD. Keeping the rules of the DTD in a separate file that all the documents can reference, rather than entering the same declarations over and over locally in each document, proves more efficient.

✦ You may find your document-authoring needs met in a public DTD. Others have already written, tested, and revised such a DTD. By referencing a public DTD, you may save a lot of time in creating a new one from scratch. DTD authors may update public DTDs from time to time, and since XML documents process any referenced external DTD subsets, you get the benefit of having your documents and document information upgraded automatically.

✦ You want your documents to be brief and easy to write, and you don't want to worry about writing or including all the necessary declarations within the prolog of the document. You can set up an efficient publishing system as long as you use a well-written, stable, and time-tested external DTD subset.

✦ You're concerned about validity. Validating XML processors are less likely to find errors if you use a well-written, stable, and time-tested external DTD subset than if you quickly whip up a bunch of local declarations. (You can quickly whip up an external DTD, too, so make sure that the one you're using is well-composed and documented.)

These are some good reasons, indeed; so the next question naturally is, why would you want to use an internal DTD subset when referencing an external one provides so many advantages? The flip side of the comprehensive external DTD subset is the brevity and pragmatic nature of the local DTD. Specifically, some advantages of using only a local DTD include the following:

✦ A single XML document, with a local DTD, can be complete, valid, and self-contained all by itself. You can transfer this document anywhere by itself, and any XML processor can process it completely without an accompanying external DTD subset file.

✦ If an external DTD subset is not necessary, it wastes time and bandwidth for the XML processor to read and process it along with your document. You can make the process more efficient by including all the necessary declarations within the document itself, so that the XML processor reads only one file instead of two (the document and the DTD).

✦ If you're not concerned with validity, going without a DTD entirely is easier and faster. As long as your document is well-formed, a nonvalidating XML processor has no trouble reading and processing the document. This is a quick-and-dirty approach to using XML.

Using a local DTD and referencing an external DTD subset are not mutually exclusive. You can do both. If you do use both subsets, keep in mind that the internal one has precedence over the external; technically, the XML processor always processes the internal DTD subset first and remembers all the declarations from it while reading the external DTD subset.

Valid XML

If an XML document is correct — meaning that it follows all the rules of both XML and its own DTD — then it is *valid* and conforms to three general rules:

✦ It's a well-formed XML document; that is, it obeys all the rules in the XML Specification, including

- Valid element sequence and nesting.

- The presence of required attributes.

- The correct type of attribute values.

✦ It has a corresponding DTD, either an internal DTD subset, external DTD, or both.

✦ It complies with the rules specified by the associated DTD(s).

While a well-formed document obeys only the rules in the XML Specification, a valid document must do this as well as be consistent within itself. Therefore, all valid XML documents are well-formed, but not all well-formed documents are valid.

Chapter 5 of *XML For Dummies* contains much more information about valid versus well-formed in XML lingo. For detailed information about well-formedness in this book, *see also* "Well-formed XML documents" in this part.

The XML Specification details all the rules for validity, so for a full listing, check the XML Specification online at www.w3.org/XML/.

An example of a well-formed document looks like this:

```
<?xml version="1.0"?>
<document>This is a well-formed
    document.</document>
```

An even simpler well-formed document looks like this:

```
<document>This is a well-formed
    document.</document>
```

Neither of these documents are valid, because

✦ No document type — either a complete internal DTD subset or a reference to an external DTD — is specified.

✦ The root element, in this case document, is not specified.

In contrast, here's an example of a valid document, which is naturally also a well-formed document:

```
<?xml version="1.0"?>
<!DOCTYPE text [
```

```
<!ELEMENT text (#PCDATA)>
]>
<text>This is a well-formed docu-
    ment.</text>
```

Notice that both of the problems mentioned earlier have been solved in this simple, but valid, document.

To tell that the document is well-formed, the XML processor simply scans the document and signals any XML errors. But how does the XML processor determine whether a document is valid? The processor does this by reading the entire document type declaration, which includes both the internal DTD subset and any external DTDs referenced within the document.

Sometimes you don't need your documents to be valid, such as in these cases:

✦ Your current application does not need a DTD to be delivered with a document; for example:

  • When your document is so simple that it doesn't require a DTD, and it wastes time and bandwidth to read one.

  • When you use a specialized XML application that automatically recognizes certain elements that you use in a particular situation, such as a department within a company that generates the same type of forms over and over.

✦ When you use a nonvalidating XML processor, which only checks the document for well-formedness.

A validating XML processor checks your document for both well-formedness and validity. If your document contains any violations of the validity constraints described by the XML Specification, the XML processor may report these errors to you, depending on which processor you use.

Because XML is a subset of SGML, any valid XML document is automatically a conforming SGML document. This is important to remember when you work with both XML and SGML.

If you looked at the XML Specification, you probably came across some codes at the end of rules that look like this:

```
[ VC: . . . ]
```

This code denotes a validity check or constraint, which is identified by name. A validity constraint in any XML Specification rule applies to all valid XML documents.

Here's an example of a validity constraint in a rule for a document type declaration:

```
doctypedecl ::= '<!DOCTYPE' S
    Name (S ExternalID)? S? ('['
    (markupdecl | PEReference |
    S)* ']' S?)? '>' [vc: Root
    Element Type]
```

This validity constraint indicates that the Name in the document type declaration must match the element type of the root element.

An example of a document that violates the validity constraint looks like this:

```
<?xml version="1.0"?>
<!DOCTYPE document [
<!ELEMENT text (#PCDATA)>
]>
<doc><text>This is a well-formed
    document.</text></doc>
```

This document produces an error in a validating XML processor because the root element, doc, does not match the Name in the document type declaration, document. In addition, neither doc nor document is declared as an element.

To fix this problem, you must do two things:

✦ Change either the Name in the document type declaration or the root element so that they match; in other words, choose either doc or document and stick with it.

✦ Declare the Name in the document type declaration as an element.

```
<?xml version="1.0"?>
<!DOCTYPE document [
<!ELEMENT document (text)>
<!ELEMENT text (#PCDATA)>
]>
<document><text>This is a valid
    document.</text></document>
```

This document is now valid and shouldn't produce an error in a validating XML processor.

Well-formed XML documents

For an XML processor to process a document correctly, the document must be *well-formed*. Well-formed documents conform to the rules of XML grammar. Some of these rules include the following:

- ✦ The document may only contain sequences of markup characters that can be parsed.

- ✦ The entire content of the document must be surrounded by a single outermost element, which is the root element or document element.

- ✦ Parameter entity references are only found in allowed places and don't consist of only part of a markup declaration.

- ✦ No attribute may appear more than once on the same start-tag.

- ✦ String attribute values cannot contain references to external entities.

- ✦ You must properly nest tags. One pair of matching start- and end-tags must not overlap another.

- ✦ You must declare parameter entities before using them.

- ✦ You must declare all entities except the typical five (`amp` or `&`, `lt` or `<`, `gt` or `>`, `apos` or `'`, and `quot` or `"`).

- ✦ You can use a binary entity only in an attribute declared as `ENTITY` or `ENTITIES`; you can't reference it in the content.

- ✦ Neither text nor parameter entities are recursive, directly or indirectly. (That is, you must not tell the XML processor to enter text or an entity into itself over and over.)

- ✦ Entity names must appear exactly as declared; this includes the letter case.

By definition, if a document is not well-formed, it's not XML.

Because XML is a subset of SGML, any well-formed XML document is automatically an SGML document. This is important to remember when you work with both XML and SGML.

If you looked at the XML Specification, you probably came across some codes at the end of rules that look like this:

```
[ WFC: . . . ]
```

This code denotes a well-formedness check or constraint, which is identified by name. A well-formedness constraint in any XML Specification rule applies to all well-formed XML documents.

An example of a well-formedness constraint in a rule for an element looks like this:

```
element ::= EmptyElemTag | STag
    content ETag [wfc: Element
    Type Match]
```

This well-formedness constraint indicates that the Name in an element's end-tag must match the element type in the start-tag.

If your document violates any of the well-formedness constraints in the XML Specification, you get a *fatal error*. When you get a fatal error, the XML processor detects and reports it to the XML application. Some processors may continue processing the data to search for further errors and report them to the application. The important thing is, once the processor detects a fatal error, the processor doesn't continue normal processing, and you have to fix the document to conform to the XML Specification.

Another way to think of well-formedness is as a collection of well-formed data objects. An entire XML document, basically a larger textual object, is well-formed if the components of data inside it are well-formed, such as

✦ As a whole, the document matches the root or document element.

✦ Each data object within the document meets all the well-formedness constraints of the XML Specification.

✦ All the parsed entities within the document are well-formed.

✦ For all non-root elements, if the start-tag is in the content of another element, the end-tag is in the content of the same element. In other words, the elements, delimited by start- and end-tags, nest properly within each other.

This is incorrect, because the tags aren't nested properly:

```
<b><i>This text is both bold and italic.</b></i>
```

To fix this, simply reverse the order of the two end-tags:

```
<b><i>This text is both bold and italic.</i></b>
```

Now the italic tags are nested properly within the <b> tags.

In this example, the order in which you should nest the tags within each other does not matter. For instance, this would work just as well:

```
<i><b>This text is both bold and italic.</b></i>
```

The result is the same: As long as you nest the tags properly, the text within the markup tags appears both bold and italic.

Note that for your document to be valid, the tags must nest in a particular order, as specified in the DTD.

In this snippet of XML document code

```
<list>
<item>first item</item>
<item>first item </item>
<item>first item </item>
</list>
```

you can see why the `<item>` tags nest inside the `<list>` tags. The `<list>` tags mark the beginning and end of the entire list, whereas the `<item>` tags mark each individual item within the list.

Turning it around just doesn't make any sense:

```
<item>
<list>first item</list>
<list>first item </list>
<list>first item </list>
</item>
```

However, this example is perfectly well-formed, because it conforms to all the rules in the XML Specification concerning well-formedness. Without seeing declarations for these elements that specify nesting order, it's impossible to tell whether this example is valid.

For more information about nesting, ***see also*** Part IV. You can find more information on validity in the "Valid XML" subsection of the "DTD Design for Effectiveness" section earlier in this part.

Markup Design

If character data makes up the content of an XML document, then markup provides the instructions for the XML processor. Much of the design of XML DTDs focuses on creating efficient and useful markup.

The components of markup include:

- ✦ Start-tags
- ✦ End-tags
- ✦ Empty elements
- ✦ Entity references
- ✦ Character references
- ✦ Comments
- ✦ CDATA section delimiters
- ✦ Document type declarations
- ✦ Processing instructions

For an explanation of start-tags, end-tags, and empty elements, *see also* Part IV; and *see also* my explanation of entity references and character references in Part V.

CDATA sections

Sometimes, you may need to use characters that are usually associated with markup as part of the literal content of a document. Of course, you can do this by using escape sequences, such as `&amp;` for the ampersand (&) or `&lt;` for the less-than sign (<). You can also use a character data section — technically, a CDATA section — to tell the XML parser to ignore markup characters.

The syntax for specifying a CDATA section looks like this:

```
<![CDATA[ the literal string ]]>
```

You can include a CDATA section anywhere you see regular character data in the text of the document.

One important use for this option is in documents containing mathematical equations and data. If you need to display this string

```
a <= b
```

in your document without the less-than sign being interpreted as a markup character, you have to include the CDATA section

```
<![CDATA[a <= b]]>
```

in your document.

Another case in which you might want to use a CDATA section is when you need to display the literal text of markup within a document — for example, a tutorial on using markup tags. If you want to display the following text in such a document

```
<markup>This text is surrounded by markup tags</
    markup>
```

the literal < and > characters should appear as they are and not be misinterpreted as part of markup instructions themselves. To do this, simply specify the CDATA section:

```
<![CDATA[<markup>This text is surrounded by markup
    tags</markup>]]>
```

You need to keep in mind one important exception to the strings of characters you can specify in a CDATA section: You can't use the string `]]>`. Examining the relevant rules in the XML Specification can help you understand why.

A set of four rules in the XML Specification describes how CDATA sections work:

```
CDSect ::= CDStart CData CDEnd
CDStart ::= '<![CDATA['
CData ::= (Char* - (Char* ']]>' Char*))
CDEnd ::= ']]>'
```

Here's what all that means:

+ The first rule says that a character data section, `CDSect`, must begin with the opening CDATA section delimiter, `CDStart`, followed by the character data of your choice, or `CData`, and then close with the end-delimiter, `CDEnd`.

+ The second rule indicates that the literal string that makes up the start-delimiter is `<![CDATA[`.

+ The expression for the third rule, `(Char* - (Char* ']]>' Char*))`, indicates that you can have zero or more of any character, except for the literal string `]]>`; see the fourth rule for why you can't use `]]>`.

+ `]]>` must be the end-delimiter for a CDATA section; therefore, it can't make up the literal string specified by the CDATA section.

According to the XML Specification, comments are not recognized in CDATA sections. You won't really have any reason to specify a comment in a CDATA section, anyway; comments are recognized on their own. If you include a comment in a CDATA section, the literal string `<!--comment-->` passes to the XML application in the same way a comment normally does.

Another thing to keep in mind is that CDATA sections can't nest; in other words, you can only use one CDATA section at a time, and you can't include one CDATA section within another.

Comments

In some cases, you may need to include text in your DTD or document that you can read later but is invisible to an XML application. You can use the comment tag to do this. Put another way, *comments* are text that only those who look at the code of the DTD can see; those looking at the document through an XML application won't see the comment text.

The syntax of a comment looks like this:

```
<!--comment-->
```

Specifically, the `<!--` is the start-delimiter markup and the `-->` is the end-delimiter markup. Anything in between these delimiters makes up the text of the comment. Neither the delimiters nor the comment text appears in the document when viewed through an XML application.

Two examples of comments follow:

```
<!--This is a comment on its own line.-->
<markup>Here is some marked-up text.</markup> <!--
    You can put a comment here, too.-->
```

You don't have to keep a long comment all on one line. A single comment can encompass several lines:

```
<!--Line one of one comment
Line two of the same comment
Line three
Last line-->
```

Just make sure to start and end the comments with the proper delimiters.

You can include any character data, including characters normally reserved for markup purposes, in the text of a comment except for the literal string `--`.

This rule in the XML Specification describes how a comment works:

```
Comment ::= '<!--' ((Char - '-') | ('-' (Char - '-
    ')))* '-->'
```

Note that you can include a single minus-sign (`-`) character, but not a double-minus-sign literal string.

For more information on notation, ***see also*** "Notation in XML Rules" in Part II. I explain the rule for `Char` in the "Characters" section of this part.

For example, this is a legal XML comment:

```
<!--My favorite characters include <,?,>, and &.-->
```

But this is not:

```
<!--I also like the double-minus-sign: --, even
    though it's not legal in the text of a com-
    ment.-->
```

You can place comments between markup anywhere in your document or DTD except before the XML declaration.

You can see a smattering of comments throughout this short document:

```
<?XML version="1.0"?>
<!DOCTYPE coolstuff SYSTEM "coolstuff.dtd"[
<!--It's OK to put a comment here-->
<!Element cooltext (#PCDATA)>
<!--and here-->
]>
<!--Wherever you want-->
<cooltext>This is a section of cooltext.</cooltext>
<!--Comments are cool!-->
```

Processing instructions

Sometimes, you may need to send a *processing instruction* — or PI — to the XML application; you can include such an instruction in a DTD or document.

Processing instructions are similar to comments in that they are not textually part of the XML document. The functional difference between a PI and a comment is that an XML processor must send a PI to an application, whereas the XML processor tells the application to ignore comments.

A PI looks like this:

```
<?name pidata?>
```

The name is called the *PI target,* which the application uses to identify a particular PI. The application recognizes only the PI targets you include in your DTD or document; the application ignores any other PIs, such as those in other DTDs.

You must include the name of the PI target; you may include data within the PI (pidata) or leave it out.

You may declare the name of the PI target as a notation to technically identify that target to the application.

See also Part V for more on notation declarations.

As long as the syntax is correct, you may use any name of a PI target you wish, except for one that begins with XML itself. This includes any combination of uppercase and lowercase letters of XML, such as xml, Xml, or xMl. Names beginning with anything that matches (('X'|'x')('M'|'m')('L'|'l')) are reserved for standardization in the current or future World Wide Web Consortium XML Specification.

The main reason the Consortium reserves the characters (('X'|'x')('M'|'m')('L'|'l')) is that XML itself uses PIs. You may often see this common example of an XML-specific PI:

```
<?XML version="1.0"?>
```

The Name and PI target is `XML`.

These two rules in the XML Specification define the syntax of a PI and a PI target:

```
PI ::= '<?' PITarget (S (Char* - (Char* '?>'
    Char*)))? '?>'
PITarget ::= Name - (('X' | 'x') ('M' | 'm') ('L' |
    'l'))
```

The first rule for PI indicates that after the `<?` start-delimiter, the name of the PI target (`PITarget`) may be followed by a white space and a set of characters, except for the literal string `?>`. The `?>` end-delimiter must close the PI.

The rule for the PI target (`PITarget`) is a regular `Name` without any letter case combination of the literal string `XML`. (***See also*** my explanations of the rule for `Name` in "Syntactic Constructs" in Part II.)

Prolog and Document Type Declaration (DTD)

In a generic sense, an XML document consists of two types of information: a variety of textual content and the instructions for those pieces of content. The instructions appear as markup.

One reason why XML is so flexible is that you can define most of your own markup and create a variety of tags that perform a wide range of functions. How the tags work and what they do is up to you; to get them to work properly requires an understanding of markup rules and syntax — in essence, knowing how to program them.

Therefore, you must somehow define the markup itself. This is where the rules of the *document type declaration* come in; these rules define the various types of markup that you may have in your document. In other words, the document type declaration contains instructions for the instructions for your document's content.

Take this section of an XML document:

```
<section><cooltext>This is the
    first sentence in this sec-
    tion, and it is cool.
    </cooltext>
This text is no longer cool.
    </section>
```

As far as XML is concerned, this document is correct: The markup tags are syntactically legal, and the two sets of markup tags are nested properly. Without a definition of the markup tags, however, you can't tell how the content within the tags appears and functions. For XML to be effective, you must define the markup by document type declaration rules.

Sometimes, the rules of a document type declaration are simply called *declarations*. These declarations define the technical instructions for markup. Among other things, defining the markup imposes constraints on how you should sequence and nest tags, such as those in the previous example. Since you can have many types of declarations in the document type declaration, many of the rules in the XML Specification are devoted to declarations.

Here are four kinds of declarations in XML:

+ **Element declarations,** which make up the logical structure of a document

+ **Attribute-list declarations,** which define and constrain elements

+ **Entity declarations,** consisting of parameter entities and general entities, which make up the physical structure of a document

+ **Notation declarations,** which define formats for referring to external binary, non-XML entities

These declarations describe how the document and its markup function. It makes sense, therefore, that you find them before the textual content of the document. The section that occurs before the textual content, or document proper, is called the *prolog*.

In this short XML section:

```
<?XML version="1.0"?>
<!DOCTYPE coolstuff SYSTEM
    "coolstuff.dtd"[
<!--comment about coolstuff-->
<!Element cooltext (#PCDATA)>
]>
<coolstuff><cooltext>This is the
    beginning of the cooltext
    document proper.</cooltext>
    </coolstuff>
```

Everything between the first line, which is the initial processing instruction, up to and including the line containing just]> is the prolog of the document.

You can include any of the following in the prolog:

+ An XML declaration (optional, but encouraged)

+ A document type declaration that may contain one or a number of rules

✦ Comments

✦ White space

✦ Processing instructions

To strictly conform to good XML style, you should begin XML documents with an *XML declaration,* which specifies the version of XML you're using.

For example:

```
<?XML version="1.0"?>
```

The declaration begins and ends with an angle bracket (< for beginning or > for ending) and a question mark (?) on the interior side of the angle bracket. Other than that, it contains the type of document it is (XML) and the version number of XML.

Note that the preceding example refers to XML version 1.0. Currently, every XML declaration should contain this statement, along with this version number, because the XML Working Group — the committee that oversees the development of the XML Specification — decided that the current specification is the first complete draft of XML. Including the version number 1.0 indicates to the XML processor that your document conforms to this version of the specification; if a document uses the value 1.0 when it doesn't conform to this version, you get an error.

You should include this or a similar XML declaration (when appropriate) in even your simplest XML documents. This is a good habit to form while you learn to use XML.

Here's another XML declaration:

```
<?XML version="1.0"
    encoding="UTF-8"?>
```

Again, this XML declaration contains all the necessary information — the type (XML) and the version number (version="1.0"). The only additional information is the character encoding (UTF-8), which the XML processor uses to read the characters in the document correctly. Note that the entire XML declaration appears within question marks and the appropriate left- and right-angle brackets, respectively.

For more information about character encodings, ***see also*** Part V.

The prolog probably contains a document type declaration. Though not required, the document type declaration often includes one or a number of rules that

✦ Define markup — technically, the constraints on the logical structure.

✦ Associate attributes with the markup. (***See also*** my discussion of attributes in detail in Part IV.)

A document type declaration doesn't always have to contain rules, as in these cases:

✦ The document refers to a separate DTD and that DTD contains all pertinent instructions.

✦ No rules are necessary at all, although this is rare — and it's a bit pointless to create a full-fledged XML document without any instructions.

The document type declaration must appear before the first element — or the first markup tag — in the document.

An example of a simple document looks like this:

```
<?XML version="1.0"?>
<!DOCTYPE simpledocument SYSTEM
    "simpledocument.dtd">
<simpledocument>This is a simple
    document, and it is correct.</
    simpledocument>
```

In this example, the XML declaration comes first. The next line is the document type declaration, which doesn't contain any rules. The final line is the first element of the document; this marks the end of the prolog. The prolog in this example includes only the first two lines.

A slightly more complex document may look like this:

```
<?XML version="1.0"?>
<!DOCTYPE complexdoc SYSTEM
    "complexdoc.dtd" [
<!ELEMENT complexdoc (#PCDATA)>
]>
<complexdoc>This document is a
    bit more complex, and it is
    also correct. </complexdoc>
```

This document type declaration contains one rule. This rule, an element declaration, describes the appropriate type of content for complexdoc. When you include one or more rules in the document type declaration, place each one on a separate line and delimit the first rule with the left-square bracket ([) on the right-hand end of the line just above it and with the right-square bracket (]) and right-angle bracket (>) on a separate line just below the last rule.

You may have documents that don't require a lengthy document type declaration. In such cases, you'd include all the instructions for the document and its markup within the prolog.

For more information about element declarations, **see also** Part IV. You can find detailed information about DTDs in the section called "DTD Design for Effectiveness" earlier in this part, as well as in Chapter 5 of *XML For Dummies*.

If the document type declaration is in the document, you must list it immediately after the XML declaration; the only items in addition to the XML declaration that may precede the document type declaration are optional processing instructions and comments.

Besides serving as the container for a variety of important declarations, the document type declaration identifies the *root element* of the document. The root element is the markup that contains the content of the entire document. All XML documents must have one, and only one, root element.

In this example of an XML document

```
<?XML version="1.0"?>
<!DOCTYPE book [
<!ELEMENT book (text)>
<!ELEMENT text (#PCDATA)*>
]>
<book>
<text>This is text within the
    book.</text>
</book>
```

book is the root element of the document, so all of the content within the document proper must appear within the start-tag <book> and end-tag </book> respectively. The <text> markup tags identify content that complies with the rule for the text element. Remember, in order for the document to be valid, you must always include the markup of any existing nonroot elements (in this example, the <text> tags) and document content (such as This is text within the book.) within the root element markup tags (in this case, the <book> tags).

Chapter 6 of *XML For Dummies* covers markup in detail. For more information about elements and markup in this book, **see also** "Element declarations" and "Tags" in Part IV.

The rule for the document type declaration appears in the XML Specification like this:

```
doctypedecl  ::= '<!DOCTYPE' S
    Name (S ExternalID)? S? ('['
    (markupdecl | PEReference |
    S)* ']' S?)? '>' [vc: Root
    Element Type]
```

One of the main components of the document type declaration rule is the markup declaration rule, which looks like this:

```
markupdecl ::= elementdecl |
    AttlistDecl | EntityDecl |
    NotationDecl | PI | Comment
    [vc: Proper Declaration/PE
    Nesting] [wfc: PEs in Internal
    Subset]
```

Notice that the components of the markup declaration include the element declaration, attribute-list declaration, entity declaration, notation declaration, processing instruction, and comment. This rule, combined with the rule for the document type declaration shown earlier, indicates that you may include any of these types of markup instructions (zero or more of any component) in the document type declaration.

For more information about notation, ***see also*** Part II. You can find more information on well-formedness and validity in the "Well-formed XML documents" and "Valid XML" subsections (respectively) of the "DTD Design for Effectiveness" section earlier in this part.

Standalone Document Declaration

Sometimes, you may want to create a *standalone document declaration* — an XML document that doesn't rely on any external sources of information, such as an external DTD or an external parameter entity referenced by the internal DTD subset. This type of XML document is completely self-sufficient; that is, all of its necessary information appears within the document itself.

The rule for the standalone document declaration in the XML Specification looks like this:

```
SDDecl ::= S 'standalone' Eq "'"
    ('yes' | 'no') "'" | S
    'standalone' Eq '"' ('yes' |
    'no') '"' [ vc: Standalone
    Document Declaration]
```

This rule indicates that you may either specify the value "yes" or "no" for the standalone document declaration.

Chapter 4 of *XML For Dummies* covers how to read the XML specifications. ***See also*** Part II of this book for details on the notation of XML Specification rules.

In a standalone document declaration, the value "yes" indicates that the XML processor should ignore any markup declarations external to the document entity — either in the DTD external subset or in an external parameter entity referenced from the internal DTD subset.

An XML declaration with the standalone document declaration set to the value "yes" looks like this:

```
<?xml version="1.0"
    standalone="yes"?>
```

Conversely, setting the standalone value to "no" indicates that the XML processor may read and process any external markup declarations. An XML declaration with the standalone document declaration set to the value "no" looks very similar to the preceding XML declaration:

```
<?xml version="1.0"
    standalone="no"?>
```

Setting the value of the standalone document declaration — or *standalone status* — to "no" merely tells the XML processor that external declarations may exist. Whether or not you include references to external entities within the internal DTD subset of your document, the standalone status doesn't change.

If you have no external markup declarations, the standalone document declaration has no meaning. If you do have external markup declarations but no standalone document declaration, the XML processor assumes the value "no".

In another scenario, if you have external markup declarations but no standalone document declaration, the XML processor automatically assumes the value is "no".

The first line of a standalone document looks like this:

```
<?xml version="1.0" standalone="yes"?>
```

This is the XML declaration, which contains the standalone declaration within it.

If you want to make sure your document reads in declarations located externally, you must either set the standalone status to "no", like this:

```
<?xml version="1.0" standalone="no"?>
```

Or leave out the standalone declaration entirely:

```
<?xml version="1.0"?>
```

This is because the processor assumes that without a standalone declaration, the standalone status is "no".

Don't be lulled into skipping the standalone declaration all the time. You must set the value of the standalone document declaration to "no" in these circumstances:

✦ Your external DTD contains attribute declarations with default values that apply to elements appearing in the document.

✦ Your document contains elements that contain white space.

✦ Your document contains entities whose references appear in the document, except for the typical five entities: amp (or &), lt (or <), gt (or >), apos (or '), and quot (or ").

✦ The values of any of these attributes change when the XML processor normalizes it.

For more information about elements and attributes, ***see also*** Part IV. To find out more about entities, ***see also*** Part V. You can find more information on special characters in the subsection "Special characters" within the "Characters" section earlier in this part. You can also find detailed information about white space in the next section.

White Space

White space comprises some of the simplest content — but sometimes the most significant — that you work with. While the concept of white space is simple, you should know how it works in XML and how you can configure it for your needs.

What is white space? It's any empty space between characters. Specifically, white space may include one or more of the following:

✦ The space character (hexadecimal Unicode character #x20)

✦ The carriage return (hexadecimal Unicode character #x9)

✦ The line feed (hexadecimal Unicode character #xD)

✦ The tab character (hexadecimal Unicode character #xA)

You may combine any of these white space characters together; as a whole, a string of white space characters is called a section of white space.

The rule for white space in the XML Specification looks like this:

```
S ::= (#x20 | #x9 | #xD | #xA)+
```

It's pretty simple; you may note that you can use any of the four Unicode characters in combination, but you must use at least one. The XML Specification denotes white space as S, and you may notice S incorporated into many rules throughout the specification, since white space is an important part of creating documents and document types.

You may come across two types of white space: One type is significant and the other isn't. To configure and work with white space properly, you must know the difference between significant and insignificant white space.

Take this snippet of marked-up text:

```
<p>Grocery list:
<list>
    <item>oranges</item>
    <item>tomato sauce</item>
    <item>paper towel</item>
</list>
</p>
```

Notice that carriage returns appear between each marked-up line of text, and sections of text within other sections are indented with tab characters. The layout of this text makes it easy for you to scan, but the white space is not significant. If you removed the white space characters from between the content and the markup tags

```
<p>Grocery
    list:<list><item>oranges</
    item><item>tomato sauce</
    item><item>paper towel</
    item></list></p>
```

it would do exactly the same thing as the code with the insignificant white space. However, the code is much less clear to anyone looking at it.

Significant white space, then, should be translated from the XML document code to the delivered version of the document — that is, the document displayed through the XML application.

You'd find significant white space in these types of documents or text:

- ✦ Poetry

- ✦ Source code

- ✦ Lists

- ✦ Textual "art," in which text is arranged in certain ways to depict a picture rather than convey content

- ✦ Specifically formatted books, articles, and papers

How the XML processor deals with white space is called *white space handling*. You should know that the XML processor doesn't simply ignore white space, whether significant or not. It reads and processes all white space, along with all other characters in a document, but it flags white space and distinguishes it as insignificant immediately before or after:

✦ The separate rules within the DTD or internal DTD subset

✦ The markup tags in mixed content (content that includes both character data and markup)

So how do you tell the XML processor when and where white space is either significant or insignificant? You declare a special attribute, the xml:space attribute, within the appropriate element attribute lists.

Here's the syntax for the xml:space attribute:

```
xml:space (default|preserve)
    "value"
```

The syntax for the entire attribute list looks like this:

```
<!ATTLIST elementname xml:space
    (default|preserve) "value">
```

You must specify the value as either default or preserve. The value default signals to the XML processor to treat white space the same way the XML application normally handles it. If you wish to transfer the white space from the XML document code to the delivered document (the document displayed on the screen in the XML application), set the value to preserve.

An example of an attribute list that preserves white space in list markup looks like this:

```
<!ATTLIST list xml:space
    (default|preserve) "preserve">
```

Guessing whether the XML processor assumes white space is significant may seem confusing. To eliminate this confusion, keep this general rule in mind: White space is significant in mixed content, which is content that may contain both character data and markup, and insignificant in element content, which is the data within a single element.

When a declaration that identifies the content model of an element is missing, the XML processor assumes all white space is significant. If you need precise control over white space handling, you must provide a declaration and specify a white space attribute.

For more information about mixed content, ***see also*** the "Character data" section earlier in this chapter. For more about both mixed content and element content, ***see also*** Part IV.

For each attribute list that you declare, the white space handling you specify remains the same throughout the document unless you override it with another instance of the xml:space attribute.

The XML processor assumes that the root element of a document doesn't indicate white space handling, unless you specify it with the preceding syntax. You would only do this with certain types of documents, such as a poem, in which white space is very important.

For example, this is an attribute-list declaration for the root element `poem`:

```
<!ATTLIST poem xml:space
    (default|preserve) "preserve">
```

The document proper could look like this:

```
<poem>
In the fisherman's house,
the smell of dried fish,
and the heat.

                        A summer storm wind;
                        the white papers on the desk,
                        all blown off.

                                        One fell,-
                                        two fell,-
                                        camellias.

        A cow is lowing
        in the cow-shed,
        under the hazy moon.

                        A summer shower;
                        the rain beats
                        on the heads of the carp.

                                When I
                                looked back,
                                the man who passed
                                was lost in mist.

-  Shiki, 1869-1902
</poem>
```

In this example of a classical Japanese haiku, maintaining the white space is very important in order to convey the tone of the poem to the reader. The start-tag `<poem>` and the end-tag `</poem>`, respectively, delimit the content of the entire document. This attribute list declaration tells the XML processor that white space in the XML document code must be preserved and transferred, intact, to the delivered document (the document that you see on the screen).

You may want to check how your XML application handles white space. For example, some XML applications ignore the white-space characters after the first one within a group of white-space characters.

Part IV

Logical Structures

XML documents consist of two complementary types of information: the data that makes up a document and the way in which that data is organized and structured. The latter type of information forms the *logical structure* of the document. The logical structure is in turn composed of a variety of forms, all of which follow strict syntaxes. These forms are generically referred to as *logical structures*. Logical structures include many ways to configure and organize your documents. Once you learn the syntax of each logical structure, you're well on your way to producing effective and impressive XML documents.

In this part . . .

- ✔ **Designing and declaring attributes**

- ✔ **Applying attributes to elements**

- ✔ **Making your documents more efficient by using conditional sections**

- ✔ **Declaring and using elements**

- ✔ **Understanding content models, element content, and mixed content**

- ✔ **Using tags**

- ✔ **Knowing whether to use an empty-element tag or a set of start- and end-tags**

- ✔ **Nesting elements properly**

Attributes

Sometimes an element may require additional information to be associated with it or some data that describes specifically what you want the element to do. You can apply such information to an element by using an *attribute specification*. Attribute specifications are often referred to as simply *attributes*.

The XML Specification rule for an attribute looks like this:

```
Attribute ::= Name Eq AttValue [vc: Attribute Value
    Type] [wfc: No External Entity References]
    [wfc: No < in Attribute Values]
```

In the expression of this rule, `Name` is the name of the attribute, `Eq` represents the equals sign (=), and `AttValue` is the attribute value, or the data description associated with the attribute name. An attribute, therefore, is essentially a *name-value pair* that is applied to an element.

This rule has one validity constraint (`vc:`) and two well-formedness constraints (`wfc:`). Each of the constraints means the following:

✦ The validity constraint `Attribute Value Type` indicates that you must declare the attribute in the DTD. Similarly, the value that you assign to the attribute name must be valid — that is, the value must conform to the type you had declared for it.

✦ `No External Entity References` means that you can't put direct or indirect entity references to external entities in your attribute values.

✦ The well-formedness constraint `No < in Attribute Values`, in technical shorthand, means that if you use replacement text for an entity referred to directly or indirectly in an attribute value, it must not contain a left-angle bracket (<). You may, however, use the escape character sequence for the left-angle bracket, which is `&lt;`.

The XML Specification rule for an attribute value reads like this:

```
AttValue ::= '"' ([^<&"] | Reference)* '"' | "'"
    ([^<&'] | Reference)* "'"
```

This rule indicates that you may use only literal data for an attribute value. *Literal data* is any quoted string that doesn't contain the double quotes (") or apostrophes (') as delimiters for that string.

Chapter 4 of *XML For Dummies* covers how to read the XML Specification. In this book, to find more information about the XML Specification and literal data, ***see also*** Part II. To find out more about entity references, ***see also*** Part V. You can find more information on attribute types in the "Attribute types" subsection later in this section.

A few examples of what an attribute or an attribute value-pair could look like this:

```
TERM="cat"

CLASS="preface"

ID="156"

HREF="http://www.w3.org/XML/"

COLOR="black"

PERSON="Mariva H. Aviram"

SONG="'Blackbird'"

ENTREF="&reference;"
```

Although the attribute names in this example are in all uppercase letters, you may use lowercase letters for your attribute names. You must be consistent in choosing one or the other, though, and remain consistent throughout your XML use. For example, the XML processor does not see TERM the same way it sees Term. This consistency also makes your documents and DTDs easier for human eyes to scan.

If you need to specify an attribute, you include it in an element's start-tag.

In a start-tag, an attribute immediately follows the space after the name of the element:

```
<element attname="attvalue">
```

This example of a start-tag contains one attribute:

```
<termdef TERM="cat">
```

In this example, termdef is the name of the element, and TERM="cat" is the attribute name-value pair.

You aren't limited to using just one attribute name-value pair. You may use as many as you need. More than one attribute is a *set of attribute specifications*. Within a set, each attribute specification has its own name and a value. In addition, you must include a space between each attribute.

For example, this start-tag contains two attributes:

```
<termdef ID="dt-cat" TERM="cat">
```

The set of attributes in this start-tag includes `ID="dt-cat"` and `TERM="cat"`.

Keep in mind a couple of rules regarding repeating specifications. You may not assign two different values to the same attribute name within one element. This, for instance, doesn't work:

```
<person title="writer" title="programmer">
```

In this example, you can't assign the attribute `title` to both values `writer` and `programmer` in the element `person`.

You can correct this by either removing one of the attribute name-value pairs or by changing one of the attribute names from `title` to something else:

```
<person title="writer" title2="programmer">
```

In some cases, however, you may want to assign the same value to two different attribute types. If declared properly, this is entirely correct:

```
<person title="writer" role="writer">
```

You may also include attributes in empty-element tags:

```
<IMG ALIGN="left" SRC="picture.gif"/>
```

Attributes in empty-element tags follow the same rules as attributes in start-tags.

Chapter 6 of *XML For Dummies* goes into detail about XML markup. In this book, to find more information on elements, ***see also*** the "Elements" section later in this part. You can also find detailed information about tags in the section called "Tags" later in this part.

In XML, you must enclose all attribute values with a pair of quotes. You may either use double quotes (") or apostrophes ('), but you must use a matching pair. If you need to include quotation marks or apostrophes in the attribute value itself, you may use the escape character sequences " or ', respectively.

In XML, you cannot include any white space between the attribute name, the equals sign, and the attribute values. All three parts of an attribute butt up together.

Wrong:

```
TERM = "cat"
```

Right:

```
TERM="cat"
```

It's a small rule to remember, but it can mean the difference between a valid document and one that produces errors.

Attribute defaults

You can avoid entering an attribute name-value pair into an element by specifying an *attribute default,* or *default value.* While you specify attribute values in the element's start-tag, default values are inherited from the DTD.

For each attribute, you may choose between one of four possible default values:

+ #REQUIRED, which means that you must include the attribute in every occurrence of the element. If the attribute is missing, the document is invalid.

+ #IMPLIED, which means that you don't have to include an attribute value, and that you didn't provide a default value. In this case, if you don't specify a value, the processor proceeds without issuing an error.

+ A specific value consisting of any string of character data that you explicitly declare in quotes. If you leave out an attribute in an associated element, the element inherits the default value that you specified.

+ #FIXED, which precedes a specific value consisting of any string of character data that you explicitly declare in quotes. In this case, any attribute value that you specify in an associated element must match the default value, or the document is invalid. You can use fixed attributes to associate semantics with an element.

This is how the rule for default values appears in the XML Specification:

```
Default ::= '#REQUIRED' | '#IMPLIED' | (('#FIXED'
    S)? AttValue) [vc: Attribute Default Legal]
    [wfc: No < in Attribute Values ]
```

This rule involves the following two constraints:

+ The validity constraint (vc:) Attribute Default Legal means that the declared default value must be legal; that is, it must meet the lexical constraints of the declared attribute type.

+ The well-formedness constraint (wfc:) No < in Attribute Values, in technical shorthand, means that if you use replacement text for an entity referred to directly or indirectly in an attribute value, it must not contain a left-angle bracket (<). You may, however, use the escape character sequence for the left-angle bracket, which is <.

This set of attribute-list declarations includes examples of each of the four types of attribute defaults:

```
<!ATTLIST termdef
     id        ID        #REQUIRED
     name      CDATA     #IMPLIED>
<!ATTLIST snack
     fruit     (orange|apple|banana) "banana">

<!ATTLIST form
     method    CDATA     #FIXED "POST">
```

In the attribute-list declaration for the element `termdef`, the value for the `id` attribute is required, but the value for `name` is optional. In the attribute-list declaration for the element `snack`, you can choose between specifying `orange`, `apple`, or `banana`, and if you do not specify one of these fruits, `snack` defaults to `banana`. Lastly, the attribute-list declaration for the element `form` indicates that if you specify a value, the value must be `POST`.

Attribute-list declarations

To tell the XML processor which attributes you want to assign to elements and how they should be used, you include an *attribute declaration* in the DTD. Specifically, attribute declarations identify

+ The elements that may have attributes.

+ The attributes, each specified by name, assigned to the elements.

+ The attribute types.

+ The value or set of values that may be associated with the attributes.

+ The default value for each attribute.

You may specify more than one attribute for an element, or a *list* of attributes, by including an *attribute-list declaration* in the DTD. In XML, you use an attribute-list declaration to declare both a single attribute and a list of attributes. Whether you specify a single attribute or a list of attributes, you declare each attribute with three parts:

+ A name

+ A type

+ A default value

The set of rules for attribute-list declarations appears like this in the XML Specification:

```
AttlistDecl ::= '<!ATTLIST' S Name AttDef* S? '>'
```

```
AttDef ::= S Name S AttType S Default
```

According to these rules for an attribute-list declaration,
`AttlistDecl` and an attribute definition, `AttDef`:

+ You must begin an attribute-list declaration with the literal
  string `<!ATTLIST`, followed by a white space (`S`).

+ After the white space, indicate the type of element with its
  `Name`. (Note: Some XML processors may issue a warning if you
  declare attributes for an element type that is itself not
  declared.)

+ You may include zero or more attribute definitions, as indicated by the asterisk (`*`).

+ An attribute definition must begin with a white space, followed by the `Name` of the attribute, the attribute type
  (`AttType`), another white space, and the attribute default
  (`Default`), respectively.

For more information about the XML Specification, *see also* Part II.
You can find more on attribute types in the "Attribute types"
subsection of this section in this part. You can also find detailed
information about attribute defaults in the section "Attribute
defaults" earlier in this part.

A typical attribute-list declaration looks like this:

```
<!ATTLIST BILL
NAME ID #REQUIRED
DATE CDATA #IMPLIED
STATUS (PAID | OUTSTANDING) 'OUTSTANDING'>
```

In this example, the `BILL` element has three attributes:

+ `NAME`, which is an `ID` attribute type and whose default is
  `REQUIRED`.

+ `DATE`, which is a string of character data (`CDATA`) and isn't
  required, as denoted by the default `IMPLIED`.

+ `STATUS`, which must be either `PAID` or `OUTSTANDING`, and
  defaults to `OUTSTANDING` if not specified.

This example may appear as a declaration in the prolog of a
document:

```
<?XML version="1.0"?>
<!DOCTYPE account SYSTEM "account.dtd" [
<!ELEMENT account (#PCDATA)*>
<!ATTLIST BILL
    NAME ID #REQUIRED
    DATE CDATA #IMPLIED
    STATUS (PAID | OUTSTANDING) 'OUTSTANDING'>
]>
```

In this example, you may have noticed that the attribute-list declaration is the longest and most complicated declaration in the prolog! This is not unusual, since so many variables can occur in an attribute-list declaration.

Keep in mind that when you provide more than one attribute-list declaration for one element type, the XML processor merges the contents of all the attribute-list declarations for that element type. In addition, if you provide more than one definition for the same attribute of an element type, the processor obeys the first declaration and ignores later declarations. Some XML processors may in fact issue a warning if you provide more than one attribute-list declaration for an element type, or if you provide more than one attribute definition for an attribute. So, in your DTD, you should provide

✦ At most one attribute-list declaration for each element type.

✦ At most one attribute definition for each attribute name.

✦ At least one attribute definition in each attribute-list declaration.

As long as the syntax is correct, you may use any attribute Name that you wish, except for those beginning with XML itself. This includes any combination of uppercase and lowercase letters of XML, such as xml, Xml, or xMl. Names beginning with anything that matches (('X'|'x')('M'|'m')('L'|'l')) are reserved for standardization in the current or future World Wide Web Consortium XML Specification.

Attribute types

When you declare an attribute or an attribute list, you specify the function of each attribute with an _attribute type_. To produce a valid document, all of the values for each attribute must be the correct type; that is, they must match what you declared for them.

Many attribute types exist and can be classified into one of three categories:

✦ String types

✦ Tokenized types

✦ Enumerated types

In the XML Specification, the rule for attribute types reads like this:

```
AttType ::= StringType | TokenizedType |
    EnumeratedType
```

The logical "or" (|) between each category of attribute types indicates that the attribute type, or AttType, must be exactly one of the three listed.

For more information about the XML Specification, *see also* Part II of this book or Chapter 4 of *XML For Dummies*.

A *string type* accepts any literal string of text, or character data (CDATA), as its value. You declare string types with the literal CDATA. CDATA values are case sensitive; so they must match the declared values exactly. You may find that you use string type attributes more than any other attribute type.

In the XML Specification, this is the rule for a string type:

```
StringType ::= 'CDATA'
```

If this is your attribute-list declaration:

```
<!ATTLIST BOOK
TITLE CDATA #IMPLIED
AUTHOR CDATA #IMPLIED>
```

Then both the TITLE and the AUTHOR attributes are string types. You may use any literal string as the value of these attributes, such as in this start-tag for a BOOK element:

```
<book title="XML For Dummies Quick Reference"
    author="Mariva H. Aviram">
```

The XML parser gets confused if you attempt to put quotes (either double quotes or apostrophes) within the literal string of a CDATA-type attribute. To avoid this problem, use the escape character sequences " for double quotes and ' for apostrophes.

Be sure not to confuse CDATA attributes with CDATA sections. In CDATA attributes, the XML processor recognizes markup and expands entity references.

For more information about characters and CDATA sections, *see also* Part III. You can find more on attribute declarations in the "Attribute-list declarations" subsection earlier in this section.

A *tokenized type* can be any of four specific types (with a total of seven type attributes):

✦ *IDentifier*, or ID, which uniquely identifies an individual element in a document, so each element can have only a single ID attribute. Since each ID is unique, all of the ID values in a document must differ. The value of an ID attribute must be a Name. Also, you must declare an ID attribute with a default of #IMPLIED or #REQUIRED. You may find that the Name of an ID attribute is usually ID.

✦ *ID reference,* or IDREF or IDREFS, which is a pointer or a set of pointers to an ID attribute value. An IDREF attribute's value is the value of a single ID attribute of an element in the document. If you need to include more than one ID reference, use IDREFS with multiple values separated by white spaces.

✦ *Entity name,* or ENTITY or ENTITIES, which is a pointer or set of pointers to an external entity. The value of an ENTITY attribute is the Name of an entity, which is case-sensitive to match the name of an external binary general entity declared in the DTD. If you need to include more than one entity reference, use ENTITIES with multiple values separated by white spaces.

✦ *Name token,* or NMTOKEN or NMTOKENS, whose value is a mixture of name characters. Name token attributes are similar to string type attributes, but they are more restricted. In general, an NMTOKEN attribute consists of a single name, as opposed to the literal string of a CDATA attribute, which could contain white spaces and other characters. Other than this restriction, you may select any name you wish for an NMTOKEN attribute, as long as it matches the NMTOKEN — although it does not have to match another attribute or declaration. If you need to include more than one name token, use NMTOKENS with multiple values separated by white spaces.

For more information about name tokens, ***see also*** Part II. To find out more about white space, ***see also*** Part III. For more on entities, check out Part V. You can find more information on attribute defaults in the "Attribute defaults" subsection earlier in this section.

In the XML Specification, the set of rules for tokenized types looks like this:

```
TokenizedType ::= 'ID'
          [vc: ID]
          [vc: One ID per Element Type]
          [vc: ID Attribute Default]
        | 'IDREF'   [vc: IDREF]
        | 'IDREFS'     [vc: IDREF]
        | 'ENTITY'     [vc: Entity Name]
        | 'ENTITIES'   [vc: Entity Name ]
        | 'NMTOKEN'    [vc: Name Token ]
        | 'NMTOKENS'   [vc: Name Token]
```

I explain all you need to know about the associated validity constraints (vc:) in the earlier descriptions of tokenized types.

Here are attribute-list declarations for two of the above-mentioned tokenized attribute types along with their corresponding start-tags:

ID attribute type:

```
<!ATTLIST DATA
ID ID #REQUIRED>
```

```
<DATA ID="123">
```

ENTITY attribute type:

```
<!ATTLIST IMG SRC ENTITY #REQUIRED>
```

```
<IMG SRC="image.gif"/>
```

The third group of attribute types, *enumerated attribute types,* enables you to specify a value taken from a list of names.

An easy way to remember what enumerated types are and what they do is knowing that each of the possible values is explicitly *enumerated* in the declaration.

You can specify one of two kinds of enumerated types: *notation types,* which enable you to choose from a set of notations that you declare in the DTD, and *general purpose enumeration,* which consists of a set of NMTOKEN tokens.

```
EnumeratedType ::= NotationType | Enumeration
```

```
NotationType ::= 'NOTATION' S '(' S? Name (S? '|'
    Name)* S? ')' [vc: Notation Attributes]
```

```
Enumeration ::= '(' S? Nmtoken (S? '|' S? Nmtoken)*
    S? ')' [vc: Enumeration]
```

A notation type attribute looks like this:

```
NOTATION ( notationA | notationB | notationC | ... )
```

Where notationA, notationB, and notationC are names of notations declared in the DTD.

Enumeration attributes look like this:

```
( NmtokenA | NmtokenB | NmtokenC )
```

You can use this example to specify a range of possible text formats:

```
NOTATION ( DOC | TXT | RTF )
```

The values of notation type attributes must match one of the notation names DOC, TXT, or RTF.

In an attribute-list declaration, you'd include this notation type like this:

```
<!ATTLIST TEXT
FORMAT NOTATION ( DOC | TXT | RTF ) "TXT">
```

This enumeration attribute specifies a choice of cities:

```
( CHICAGO | DALLAS | INDIANAPOLIS | SAN_FRANCISCO )
```

The values of these attributes must match one of these NMTOKEN tokens.

In an attribute-list declaration, you'd include this enumeration type like this:

```
<!ATTLIST location
CITY ( CHICAGO | DALLAS | INDIANAPOLIS |
    SAN_FRANCISCO )"CHICAGO">
```

To avoid confusion and redundancy, don't list the same NMTOKEN more than once in the enumerated attribute types of a single element type.

Attribute-value normalization

One quirk of XML is that validating XML processors massage the data that you supply in your attribute value; that is, the processor changes the data a little bit before passing it to the XML application. This process of massaging the data is called *normalization*.

Normalizing the data of attribute values involves these procedures:

✦ Replacing strings that mark line endings or boundaries in the attribute value and in any entities referred to in it with a single space character (hexadecimal code #x20).

✦ Expanding character references and internal parsed entity references.

✦ If the attribute is not of type CDATA, reducing all strings of white space to single space characters and removing leading and trailing white space.

For more information about characters and white space, *see also* Part III. To find out more about entities, *see also* Part V. You can find more information on attribute types in the "Attribute types" subsection earlier in this section.

Conditional Sections

You may run into situations in which you need to use both internal and external DTD subsets. The internal and external DTD subsets should complement each other; that is, some necessary declarations may be in the external DTD subset while you include additional information locally within the prolog of the document. Sometimes, however, instructions in the internal DTD subset conflict with those in the external DTD subset. One solution to this problem is to go through both DTD subsets manually and delete the conflicting lines of code or turn them into comments. Another more flexible and savvy solution is to use a *conditional section*.

A conditional section is basically any set of markup that you include in or exclude from the logical structure of the DTD. To specify in the conditional section whether you want to include or exclude a set of markup, you must provide a keyword with a value of either INCLUDE or IGNORE, respectively.

For more information about DTDs or character data, check out Chapter 5 of *XML For Dummies; see also* Part III of this book.

The syntax for including a set of markup looks like this:

```
<![INCLUDE[
[included markup]
]]>
```

Similarly, this is the syntax for excluding a set of markup:

```
<![IGNORE[
[excluded markup]
]]>
```

You may also nest one conditional section within another:

```
<![INCLUDE[
[included markup]
<![IGNORE[
[excluded markup within a section of included
    markup]
]]>
]]>
```

Anything nested inside an IGNORE conditional section is ignored by the XML processor, including INCLUDE conditional sections:

```
<![IGNORE[
[excluded markup]
<![INCLUDE[
[excluded markup, even though its keyword says
    "INCLUDE"]
]]>
]]>
```

You can place a conditional section around

+ One or more complete declarations

+ Comments

+ Processing instructions

+ Nested conditional sections

+ White space, which may intermingle with any of the above

This means that you can include or exclude any combination of these types of markup in the instructions that are to be processed by the XML processor.

For more information about comments, processing instructions, and white space, **see also** Part III.

You can only use conditional sections within an external DTD subset.

This set of rules in the XML Specification governs how conditional sections work:

```
conditionalSect ::= includeSect | ignoreSect

includeSect ::= '<![' S? 'INCLUDE' S? '[' extSubset
    ']]>'

ignoreSect ::= '<![' S? 'IGNORE' S? '['
    ignoreSectContents* ']]>'

ignoreSectContents ::= Ignore ('<!['
    ignoreSectContents ']]>' Ignore)*

Ignore ::= Char* - (Char* ('<![' | ']]>') Char*)
```

This set of rules breaks down as follows:

- ✦ The first line is the overall rule for a conditional section. According to this rule, a conditional section, or conditionalSect, may apply to an included section, or includeSect, or an excluded section, ignoreSect, as indicated by the logical "or" (|).

- ✦ The second rule specifies the syntax for an included section, includeSect. If a conditional section with the keyword INCLUDE appears in the external DTD subset (extSubset), then the processor treats the contents of the conditional section as part of the document.

- ✦ The third rule specifies the syntax for an excluded section. This syntax indicates that you can use zero or more excluded section contents (ignoreSectContents), as denoted with the asterisk (*). If you use the keyword IGNORE for this purpose, the XML processor doesn't treat the contents of the conditional section as part of the document.

- ✦ The next rule indicates that the content of excluded sections may occur recursively; that is, excluded sections may appear within other excluded sections. This rule has two primary purposes:

  - • The XML processor reads the contents of ignored conditional sections — even though it doesn't do anything with these contents — to detect nested conditional sections and to detect the end of the outermost (ignored) conditional section.

- It ensures that when a conditional section with the keyword INCLUDE appears within a larger conditional section with the keyword IGNORE, the processor ignores both the outer and the inner conditional sections.

✦ The last rule dictates that you may use any character from the Unicode character set (Char) in the content of a conditional section, but you may not use the strings `<![` or `]]>`, because these strings are reserved for the syntax of the conditional section itself.

For more information about the XML Specification, read Chapter 4 of *XML For Dummies,* or **see also** Part II of this book.

You may find that you use conditional sections most often in conjunction with parameter entities. In this case, the processor replaces the parameter entity with its content before deciding whether it should include or ignore the conditional section.

An example of a conditional section with two parameter entities, manuscript and release, looks like this:

```
<!ENTITY % manuscript 'INCLUDE'>
<!ENTITY % release 'IGNORE'>

<![%manuscript;[
<!ELEMENT book (notes*, title, body, appendixes?)>
]]>
<![%release;[
<!ELEMENT book (title, body, appendixes?)>
]]>
```

In this example, the XML processor replaces the entity manuscript with `<!ELEMENT book (notes*, title, body, appendixes?)>` before it realizes that it must include it. Similarly, the processor replaces the entity release with `<!ELEMENT book (title, body, appendixes?)>` before excluding it.

For more information about parameter entities, **see also** Part V.

Elements

Like a document that conforms to any type of markup language, an XML document consists of two essential parts: data or information, and the logical units that contain the data or information. If you think of the data or information as items that you organize and store, then the logical units are the storage containers for those items. In XML, the data that makes up one virtual storage unit is an *entity,* while the logical unit of information itself is an *element.* In this way, entities and elements are integrally related, so they're easily confused.

```
<element>This sentence represents a string of data,
    or an entity. It is surrounded by "element"
    tags, which represent this entity's storage
    container.</element>
```

For more information about markup, ***see also*** Part III. To find out more about entities, check out Part V. Chapter 6 of *XML For Dummies* covers markup in detail.

Storage containers, or elements, can themselves contain smaller storage containers, or subelements. A *subelement* is the child of the element; conversely, the element is the parent of that subelement. Although a subelement is a child of another element, it's a complete element in and of itself and may itself contain other elements as well as text.

```
<element>
<subelement>The subelement is the child of the
    parent "element." </subelement>
</element>
```

Remember that all documents have at least one element, which is the root element of the document. If a document has any other elements in addition to the root element, then they're contained by another element. Specifically, a nonroot element may be contained by the root element itself or by another nonroot element. The root element is the parent of all the elements it directly contains, and those elements may similarly be parents of other element children.

Such a scenario could look like this:

```
<rootelement>
    <nonrootelement>
        <nonrootelementchild>
        <nonrootelementchild>
    </nonrootelement>
</rootelement>
```

Of course, the names of these elements are generic, and you would probably never run into such a document.

Here's a more realistic example:

```
<document>
    <section>
        <p>This is the first paragraph in a section
        of a document.
        </p>
        <p>This is the second paragraph in the same
        section of this document.
        </p>
    </section>
</document>
```

In this example, `document` represents the root element, and `section` is the child of `document`. Similarly, p is the child of the element `section`.

For more information about root elements, ***see also*** Part III. You can find more detailed information on tags in the section called "Tags" later in this part.

Although quite common, elements represented by the sets of tags in the preceding example aren't the only type of elements. Technically, elements can contain a number of things:

✦ Character data

✦ Other elements, known as subelements or children

✦ `CDATA` sections

✦ Processing instructions

✦ Comments

✦ White space

✦ Entity references

For more information about character data, `CDATA` sections, processing instructions, or comments, ***see also*** Part III.

Content models

To enable your document to be read by human eyes (and to be understood!), as well as make sure the XML application understands how the elements of your document work and what they contain, you must describe them somehow. Technically, a description of an element is its *content model*. You can also think of content models in nontechnical terms: If an element is a storage container of data, or content, then the content model describes the content inside the storage container and lists what the storage container can contain.

You find content models within element declarations, which in turn appear in a document's document type declaration.

For more information about document type declarations, check out Chapter 5 of *XML For Dummies* or ***see also*** Part III. You can find more on element content in the "Element content" subsection of this section. You can also find detailed information about element declarations in the "Element declarations" subsection of this section.

In this example of a document prolog:

```
<?xml version="1.0" encoding="UTF-8" ?>
<!DOCTYPE form [
```

```
<!ELEMENT form (name, company, IDnum, comments)>
<!ELEMENT name (#PCDATA)>
<!ELEMENT company (#PCDATA)>
<!ELEMENT IDnum (#PCDATA)>
<!ELEMENT comments (p+)>
<!ELEMENT p (#PCDATA)>
]>
```

The document type declaration consists of these element declarations:

```
<!ELEMENT form (name, company, IDnum, comments)
<!ELEMENT name (#PCDATA)>
<!ELEMENT company (#PCDATA)>
<!ELEMENT IDnum (#PCDATA)>
<!ELEMENT comments (p+)>
<!ELEMENT p (#PCDATA)>
```

In turn, these element declarations specify the following types of content, or content models, respectively:

```
(name, company, IDnum, comments)>
(#PCDATA)
(#PCDATA)
(#PCDATA)
(p+)
(#PCDATA)
```

Notice that some of the content models simply indicate character data (#PCDATA) content, while other content models refer to other elements.

Here is an example of a slightly more complex content model:

```
(body, (p | list | comment)*, section)
```

This model requires a body element, followed by zero or more p, list, or comment elements, and then followed by zero or more section elements.

Besides specifying that an element contains character data or another element, you may also specify two other content models:

✦ The literal EMPTY, which indicates that the element has no content, and the element's markup would therefore have no end-tag.

✦ The literal ANY, which indicates that any content is allowed.

The ANY content model is sometimes useful during document conversion, such as when you convert a document from SGML to XML. Typically, however, you should avoid using ANY in a production environment because it disables all content checking in the corresponding element, and a validating XML processor doesn't issue an error in such a case.

For more information on the literals EMPTY and ANY, ***see also*** the "Element declarations" subsection later in this section.

Element content

If an element type can only contain other elements, also known as subelements or child elements, then technically, it contains *element content*. Specifically, element content doesn't contain character data.

Element content is constrained by a specific type of content model, which describes the allowed types of child elements and the order in which the child elements must appear. The grammar for element content is built upon *content particles (cps),* which consist of one of the following:

✦ Names

✦ Choice lists of content particles

✦ Sequence lists of content particles

The set of rules in the XML Specification that technically describes how element content and content models work looks like this:

```
children ::= (choice | seq) ('?' | '*' | '+')?

cp ::= (Name | choice | seq) ('?' | '*' | '+')?

choice ::= '(' S? cp ( S? '|' S? cp )* S? ')' [vc:
     Proper Group/PE Nesting]

seq ::= '(' S? cp ( S? ',' S? cp )* S? ')' [vc:
     Proper Group/PE Nesting]
```

All this means that

✦ The rule for children specifies the option of using either choice or seq.

✦ The optional character following a name or list of options enables you to choose whether the element or the content particles in the list appear zero or one time (?), zero or more times (*), or one or more times (+).

✦ Similarly, the content particle, cp, provides an option of using Name, choice, or seq. You may also choose to use one of the suffix operators, ?, *, or +.

✦ Name is the type of an element that may appear as a child.

✦ The rule for choice indicates that any content particle in a choice list may appear in the element content at the corresponding location — that is, where the choice list appears in the grammar of the content model.

◆ The validity constraint (vc), Proper Group/PE Nesting, indicates that you must properly nest the parameter-entity replacement text (PE) with parenthesized groups. Specifically, if the PE contains either of the opening or closing parentheses in a choice, seq, or Mixed construct, the same replacement text must contain both parentheses.

◆ Content particles in a sequence list (seq) must each appear in the element content in the specified order of the list. The validity constraint is the same as the one in choice.

According to these rules, the element content matches a content model only if you can follow a path through the content model that conforms to the sequence, choice, and repetition operators, and that also matches any element type listed in the content model.

For more information about the XML Specification, **see also** Part II. To find out more about validity, check out Part III. You can find more on content models in the "Content models" subsection earlier in this section.

Here are a few examples of element declarations with content models that involve only element content:

```
<!ELEMENT spec (front, body, back?)>

<!ELEMENT div1 (front, (p | list | message)*,
    div2*)>

<!ELEMENT reference-body (%div.mix; | %ref.mix;)*>
```

As you may notice, all of these content models only list other elements; you find no character data ((#PCDATA)) in content models. Such content models are also known as *element-content models*.

For more information about character data, **see also** Parts III and V.

Element declarations

Once you understand what an element is and decide that you need to use one or more, how do you go about defining and configuring them for your documents? XML provides the flexible yet precise method of defining elements through *element declarations*.

Element declarations enable you to

◆ Create new elements and name them.

◆ Define elements according to your document needs; specifically, define and constrain the nature of the element content.

- ✦ Define the organization for your elements, such as which elements are parents and which are children, and how they should nest.

- ✦ Define the root element.

- ✦ Constrain the content of an element; that is, decide what content may be allowed and what is prohibited. For example, you can declare an element to have only #PCDATA or perhaps contain only one other element.

Conversely, you must declare any element that you use in your document — and properly define it through the element declaration — to produce a valid document.

According to the rule in the XML Specification, the syntax for an element declaration looks like this:

```
elementdecl ::= '<!ELEMENT' S Name S contentspec S?
    '>' [vc: Unique Element Type Declaration]
```

To understand how this works, you can break down each piece of this rule:

- ✦ All element declarations must begin with <!ELEMENT.

- ✦ A white space, S, follows <!ELEMENT.

- ✦ The Name of the element follows the white space. The Name indicates the element's *type*. Each element has such a type, which is sometimes called its *generic identifier (GI)*.

- ✦ More white space must follow the Name.

- ✦ The next item in this sequence is contentspec, which I describe a little later.

- ✦ After the contentspec, you may either include exactly one white space or leave it out, which is an option indicated by the S?.

- ✦ Finally, close the element declaration with a right-angle bracket (>).

- ✦ The validity constraint (vc:), Unique Element Type Declaration, indicates that you may not declare an element type more than once; in other words, each element type must be unique.

According to a corresponding XML Specification rule, the content specification, or contentspec, follows this syntax:

```
contentspec ::= 'EMPTY' | 'ANY' | Mixed | children
    [vc: Element Valid]
```

The rule for contentspec itself breaks down as follows:

✦ The logical "or" (|) indicates that any of the contentspec may contain any of the four options listed, 'EMPTY', 'ANY', Mixed, or children, but that you must use exactly one of the options.

✦ Using the 'EMPTY' option, you include the literal string EMPTY in your element declaration. EMPTY means that the element has no content.

✦ As an inverse rule to EMPTY, an element declaration matching the literal string ANY indicates that the element may contain any type of content, such as character data, any other element types, or a mixture of both.

✦ Mixed, a nonliteral option, enables you to include a mixture of elements and character data in your element declaration.

✦ Another nonliteral option, children, allows you to include Names of elements that are subelements, or children, of the element named in the element declaration.

✦ The validity constraint (vc:), Element Valid, indicates that an element is valid if you provide a corresponding element declaration for it. Strictly speaking — and this may seem obvious — the Name of the element must match the element type. In addition, you must properly observe all the points mentioned above for the element to be valid.

As long as the syntax is correct, you may use any element Name that you wish, except for ones that begin with XML itself. This includes any combination of uppercase and lowercase letters of XML, such as xml, Xml, or xMl. Names beginning with anything that matches (('X'|'x')('M'|'m')('L'|'l')) are reserved for standardization in the current or future World Wide Web Consortium XML Specification.

For more information about the XML Specification, including literals and Names, *see also* Part II. For more about white space, *see also* Part III.

With documents that follow a strict format, you may require your elements to be valid, and you want the XML processor to notify you if they aren't. In such a case, specifying your element declarations with as much detail as possible helps. For example, for the processor to properly validate your documents, you may constrain the structure of your elements with one or a number of attribute-list declarations. You may also configure the processor to issue a warning when a declaration mentions an element type that you haven't declared elsewhere.

Here are a few examples of element declarations:

```
<!ELEMENT hr EMPTY>

<!ELEMENT p (#PCDATA|i)*>

<!ELEMENT content (p+)>

<!ELEMENT %name.para; %content.para;>

<!ELEMENT message ANY>

<!ELEMENT section (p+, div, takeout?)>

<!ELEMENT div (#PCDATA | quote)*>
```

As you may have noted, just this sampling alone represents a wide variety of elements. Although the syntax of element declarations and the rules of element use are strict, you can do a lot with them.

For more information about notation, including suffix operators, *see also* Part II.

Now that you know how to create a variety of properly constructed element declarations, where do you put them? Like all other types of declarations, element declarations fall into the document type declaration. The document type declaration itself may be contained locally inside the prolog of the document, or it may reside in an external DTD. Where the document type declaration resides is irrelevant, as long as all the element declarations appear within it.

An example of a small document with a local document type declaration that contains one element declaration looks like this:

```
<?xml version="1.0" encoding="UTF-8" ?>
<!DOCTYPE message [
<!ELEMENT message (#PCDATA)>
]>

<message>This is my message to you.</message>
```

The only element declaration in the document type declaration is

```
<!ELEMENT message (#PCDATA)>
```

This element declaration is very simple: the Name of the element, which indicates its type, is message, and the content specification, (#PCDATA), indicates that the element message may only contain character data.

Notice that the Name of the element, message, is the same as the name of the document type declaration. This indicates that message is the Name of the root element of this document. You can see this in practice with the fact that the text of the document proper is surrounded by message start- and end-tags; this results in a simple but perfectly valid document.

For more information about character data, ***see also*** Parts III and V.

This document exemplifies a local document type declaration that contains several element declarations:

```
<?xml version="1.0" encoding="UTF-8" ?>
<!DOCTYPE message [
<!ELEMENT message (from, to, subject, date, body)>
<!ELEMENT from (#PCDATA)>
<!ELEMENT to (#PCDATA)>
<!ELEMENT subject (#PCDATA)>
<!ELEMENT date (#PCDATA)>
<!ELEMENT body (p+)>
<!ELEMENT p (#PCDATA)>
]>

<message>
<from>Mariva</from>
<to>Reader</to>
<subject>Example</subject>
<date>December 31, 1999</date>
<body>
<p>Dear Reader,</p>
<p>This is an example of how you can declare a
   number of elements in a document type declara-
   tion, and how markup tags indicate how these
   elements are used in a document.</p>
<p>Does this make sense to you now?</p>
</body>
</message>
```

In this example, many of the elements declared in the document type declaration, such as from, to, subject, and date, are very simple because they just indicate that the element contains character data. The element body may contain one or more p elements, as indicated by the content specification (p+); body is thus the parent of p. The root element, message, contains all the other elements and indicates that you must sequence these child elements in the specified order. In the document proper section, all of these elements appear in order, nest properly, and contain the correct types of content.

When creating element declarations, you must follow a few rules:

+ Do not use the ampersand (&) in the element Name.

+ Commas (,) in between items in a content list indicate that the elements must follow the order in which they appear in the list. Always use commas when you must specify a strict order of how elements must occur in your document.

✦ If your element declaration specifies mixed content, you must separate the optional content from each other with the logical "or" (|).

✦ In addition, if your element declaration specifies mixed content, then character data, or #PCDATA, must always come first.

For more information about character data, ***see also*** Parts III and V. You can find more on mixed content in the "Mixed content" subsection later in this section.

Mixed content

If a content model for an element contains both subelements (or child elements) and character data, then the content model is *mixed,* or you can say that the element contains *mixed content.* The mixture of character data and child elements may appear in any order, as long as they follow the grammar specified by the content model. Essentially, mixed content indicates that the content model in a DTD allows character data to be optionally interspersed with child elements.

While element content cannot already contain any character data, mixed content may consist of

✦ Only child elements.

✦ Only character data.

✦ A mixture of child elements and character data.

✦ An empty string of character data — that is, when a set of start- and end-tags contain nothing.

For more information about character data, ***see also*** Parts III and V. You can find more on element content in the "Element content" subsection earlier in this section. You can also find more on content models in the "Content models" subsection earlier in this section.

Take the following example:

```
<tag></tag>
```

According to the rules of mixed content listed above, this set of tags can represent mixed content containing the empty string. According to the rules of empty-element tags, however, this set of tags can also represent an empty element. The sets of tags for both circumstances look identical. To ensure the difference between mixed content with an empty string of character data and an empty element, you must specify the structure of the element in the DTD.

Chapter 5 of *XML For Dummies* covers the specifics of DTDs, and Chapter 6 covers XML tags. For more information about DTDs in this book, ***see also*** Part III. You can find more on empty elements in the "Empty-element tags" subsection of the "Tags" section later in this part.

An element declaration that specifies mixed content is a *mixed-content declaration*. The rule for mixed content appears like this in the XML Specification:

```
Mixed ::= '(' S? '#PCDATA' (S? '|' S? Name)* S?
     ')*' | '(' S? '#PCDATA' S? ')' [vc: Proper
     Group/PE Nesting] [vc: No Duplicate Types]
```

Essentially, this rule states that you may supply any mixture of character data and child element Names. Specifically:

✦ To declare a mixed-content element properly, you must place the special symbol #PCDATA (whose moniker PCDATA stands for *parseable character data*), and then optionally include child element Names interspersed with other occurrences of #PCDATA.

✦ You must separate each element in the content specification list by the logical "or" (|).

✦ The entire group of listed child elements must be optional, as indicated by the asterisk (*).

✦ The validity constraint (vc:), No Duplicate Types, indicates that the same name must not appear more than once in a single mixed-content declaration.

Here are a few examples of mixed-content declarations:

```
<!ELEMENT p (#PCDATA|a|ul|b|i|em)*>

<!ELEMENT p (#PCDATA | %font; | %phrase;
     | %special; | %form;)* >

<!ELEMENT b (#PCDATA)>
```

When using mixed content in a document, you find that while the child element types may be constrained, the order in which they appear or their number of occurrences is not.

For more information on element declarations, ***see also*** the "Element declarations" subsection earlier in this section.

Here is an example of mixed content in action — that is, the character data and markup of a document.

```
<section>
<p>Here is the first paragraph.</p>
<p>Here is the second paragraph.</p>
</section>
```

The element `section` contains mixed content that consists of both character data (`Here is the first paragraph.` and `Here is the second paragraph.`) and two instances of the child element `p`.

Tags

If elements and associated attributes make up the logical structure of XML documents, then *tags* are responsible for letting both you and the XML processor know where each element is and when and how to process it.

Technically, tags are the sections of character data that indicate markup within a document, as opposed to the character data that makes up the textual content of the document. (Not all markup appears in the form of tags, however; entity references, processing instructions, and comments are all forms of markup that don't use tags.)

If you've ever looked at an XML document, you've seen at least one set of tags. For instance, all XML documents must contain at least the root element, which is delimited by a start-tag and an end-tag. XML, in essence, is a metalanguage that provides rules defining a set of tags that you use within a document. You cannot use XML without using tags, and XML processors can't work properly without parsing tags.

What do tags do, specifically? Here are the main purposes of tags:

✦ To delimit an XML entity, which is a physical structure of an XML document.

✦ To include and specify attributes associated with an element.

✦ To delimit contents — essentially containing character data and possibly other tags.

✦ To define the syntax of an element.

The XML processor reads the tags in a document and in turn provides an XML application with access to the content delimited by the tags. The application then performs the necessary tasks on the entities.

For more information about entities, check out Part V. To find out more about XML processors and applications, ***see also*** Part I. In addition, you can find more on elements in the "Element declarations" section earlier in this part.

Now that you know what a tag is and what it does, you should know what it looks like. All tags are delimited by left-angle (<) and right-angle (>) brackets.

For more information about special characters, check out Chapter 9 of *XML For Dummies* or ***see also*** Part III.

The slash (/) also appears a lot in tags, but not always. You can find the slash immediately following the left-angle bracket or immediately preceding the right-angle bracket, depending on the type of tag you use.

Here are several examples of tags:

```
<i>
```

```
</b>
```

```
<hr/>
```

```
<br>
```

```
<font color="red">
```

```
<FORM name="Informational Form" author="Jane Doe"/>
```

Some of these tags represent incomplete entities without the presence of other tags that correspond to them. Some of these tags are also missing pertinent content.

Using the examples above, complete entities would look like this:

```
<i>This text is italicized.</i>
```

```
<b>This text is bold.</b>
```

```
<hr/>
```

```
<br></br>
```

```
<font color="red">This text appears red.</font>
```

```
<FORM name="Informational Form" author="Jane Doe"/>
```

Notice that some of these entities contain tags that appear in pairs, and others have only one tag. In addition, some, but not all, pairs of tags contain content within the sets of tag, because two types of tags exist; also, while the syntax of tags is strict, they allow for much flexibility in design.

The two types of tags are

♦ Empty-element tags.

♦ A pair of nonempty element tags. Specifically, the nonempty element tag pair consists of a start-tag marking the beginning of the entity and an end-tag marking the end.

You can find more detailed information on empty-element tags in the "Empty-element tags" subsection later in this section. For more information on start-tags and end-tags, *see also* the "Start-tags and end-tags" subsection later in this section.

Here is the rule for an element, which specifies the types and syntax of tags, as it appears in the XML Specification:

```
element ::= EmptyElemTag | STag content ETag [wfc:
    Element Type Match]
```

Because EmptyElemTag is separated from STag content ETag with the logical "or" (|), what marks an element is either an empty-element tag, or the start-tag/end-tag pair, but not both. The well-formedness constraint (wfc), Element Type Match, indicates that the Name in an element's end-tag must match the element type in the start-tag.

For more information about the XML Specification and about Names, *see also* Part II.

As long as the syntax is correct, you may use any Names for elements and subsequent tags that you wish, except for ones that begin with XML itself. This includes any combination of uppercase and lowercase letters of XML, such as xml, Xml, or xMl. Names beginning with anything that matches (('X'|'x')('M'|'m')('L'|'l')) are reserved for standard-ization in the current or future World Wide Web Consortium XML Specification.

Empty-element tags

If an element does not contain any content — that is, no subelements or character data — it's an *empty-element tag*. Empty elements don't require both start-tags and end-tags the way all other elements do. The most common way to denote an empty element is by using just one tag, an empty-element start-tag, which is slightly different from the start-tags (and end-tags) of other elements.

To find more information on element content, *see also* the "Element content" section earlier in this part.

An empty element start-tag looks like this:

```
<Name/>
```

The Name must follow the rules of XML Names. For more informa-tion about Names, *see also* Part II.

Here are two examples of empty-element tags:

```
<emptytag/>
```

```
<br/>
```

Here are two slightly more complex empty-element tags:

```
<BOOK name="XML For Dummies Quick Reference"
    author="Mariva H. Aviram"/>
```

```
<IMG align="left" src="http://www.w3.org/Icons/WWW/
    w3c_home" />
```

You may notice that the length of an empty-element tag doesn't matter, as long as it indicates an element with no content and it has the correct syntax. You may use the empty-element tag if you declare it by using the keyword EMPTY.

On first glance, the empty-element tag may seem eerily similar to the end-tag of a nonempty element, probably because both types of tags use a slash (/). You should remember that, with the end-tag of a nonempty element, the / appears immediately before the Name, whereas the / in the start-tag of the empty-element tag comes immediately afterward.

In this example of an element containing content:

```
<contenttag>This is some content.</contenttag>
```

The end-tag of this nonempty element is </contenttag>.

This empty-element tag

```
<emptytag/>
```

conforms to the rules of empty-element tags by both standing alone (in other words, not containing content) and having the / located at the end of the emptytag Name of the element.

The start-tag of an empty element, specifically the part of the tag that ends with a slash, signals to the XML processor that the element contains no other content. It's like a "hint" encoded within the element that defines this information to the XML parser. In a non-DTD, and thus nonvalidating, document, this signal or hint is necessary, because the XML processor wouldn't otherwise know whether the tag represents an element with content and whether to scan ahead in the parsing for required element content.

For more information about DTDs and validation, *see also* Part III. You can find more on attributes in the section called "Attribute-list declarations" earlier in this part. You can also find detailed information about start-tags and end-tags in "Start-tags and end-tags" later in this section.

The rule for the empty-element tag appears like this in the XML Specification:

```
EmptyElemTag ::= '<' Name (S Attribute)* S? '/>'
    [wfc: Unique Att Spec]
```

Notice that all empty-element tags look the same, with the left-angle bracket (<) before the tag and both the / and the right-angle bracket (>) immediately following it. According to this Specification rule, you may include a white space (S) before the / or leave it out. Also, you may optionally include an attribute along with the Name. The well-formedness constraint (wfc), Unique Att Spec, indicates that attribute names may not appear more than once in the same empty-element tag.

For more information about the XML Specification, ***see also*** Part II.

In the following example:

```
<BOOK name="XML For Dummies Quick Reference"
    author="Mariva H. Aviram"/>
```

BOOK is the Name of this tag, and name="XML For Dummies Quick Reference" author="Mariva H. Aviram" are two attribute name-value pairs.

Another approach, recently accepted in the XML Specification, is to represent an empty element with a start-tag immediately followed by an end-tag.

Here are two examples:

```
<emptytag></emptytag>
```

```
<br></br>
```

This approach is acceptable and correct, but it does take up slightly more space than simply using the empty-element tag.

When would you use an empty-element tag? Using an empty-element tag would be appropriate in these situations:

+ To include physical division in the document text, such as a break or horizontal rule.

+ To denote the inclusion of an image or reference to another external binary file.

+ To include a piece of information about the text without it being a container for content.

Start-tags and end-tags

Elements that contain content, either subelements or character data or both, are called *nonempty elements*. For the XML processor to know that an element contains content, as well as know when it should start and stop parsing the content, a nonempty element is delimited by a *start-tag* at the beginning of the element and an *end-tag* at the end. The beginning and the end of an element are the element's *boundaries*. A pair of start- and end-tags, therefore, mark the boundaries of an element.

To find more information on element content, **see also** the "Element content" subsection of the "Elements" section earlier in this part.

The syntax of a nonempty element looks like this:

`<Name>[content]</Name>`

You may have already guessed that `<Name>` is the start-tag and `</Name>` is the end-tag of the element that contains `content`. Generically, the content of the element is the text between the start-tag and end-tag. The `Name` of the end-tag must be identical to the `Name` of the start-tag. This `Name` must follow the rules of XML `Names`.

For more information about `Names`, **see also** Part II.

The rule for the start-tag appears like this in the XML Specification:

```
STag ::= '<' Name (S Attribute)* S? '>' [wfc:
     Unique Att Spec]
```

Similarly, the rule for the end-tag reads

```
ETag ::= </' Name S? '>'
```

According to this Specification rule, you may include a white space (S) before the closing delimiter of the tag, the right angle bracket (>), or leave it out. Also, you may optionally include an attribute along with the `Name` only in the start-tag. The well-formedness constraint (`wfc`), `Unique Att Spec`, indicates that attribute names may not appear more than once in the same start-tag.

For more information about the XML Specification, **see also** Part II. You can find more on attributes in the section called "Attribute-list declarations" earlier in this part.

Here are two examples of start-tags:

`<nonemptytag>`

`<i>`

Here are the two corresponding end-tags:

```
</nonemptytag>
```

```
</i>
```

Similarly, here are two complete examples of start-tags and end-tags surrounding nonempty elements:

```
<nonemptytag>Content goes here.</nonemptytag>
```

```
<i>This text is italicized.</i>
```

These are fairly simple uses of start-tags and end-tags.

In this example

```
<font size="3">The font of this text is size 3.
    </font>
```

`font` is the `Name` of the element, and `size="3"` is the attribute name-value pair. You may include as many attributes in your start-tag as you like, as long as each of the attribute `Names` is unique and the tag conforms to the correct syntax. Whether you include attributes in your start-tags, the start-tags and end-tags of non-empty elements always behave the same way.

Another example of a nonempty element delimited at the beginning by a start-tag containing attributes looks like this:

```
<termdef id="dt-cat" term="cat">cat</termdef>
```

This nonempty element is a convenient way of identifying and defining the term `cat` for an application that may require such a definition.

Just like with empty-element tags, you have to make sure the syntax of the tags is correct. The slash of the end-tag must appear at the beginning of the tag `Name`, or the XML parser gets confused.

To find more information on empty-element tags, ***see also*** the "Empty-element tags" subsection earlier in this section.

When would you use a start-tag and end-tag to denote a nonempty element? Here are a few situations in which using such a set of tags would be appropriate:

- ✦ To format a section of text, such as when making the text bold, italic, or underlined, or a certain font or size of text.

- ✦ To define a term with an identifier and other pertinent information about the term.

✦ To contain subelements, such as when a chapter of a book contains sections within the chapter. This includes when the root element of a document contains all other elements.

Here is an example of a nonempty element that contains a few different types of content:

```
<chapter>
<section>
This is the first line.<br/>
This is the second line.
</section>
</chapter>
```

To sort out the parts of this element, you can break the process down into pieces:

✦ Although you see two nonempty elements in this example, the main one is the content delimited by the <chapter></chapter> start-tag and end-tag pair.

✦ The nonempty element delimited by <section></section> is a subelement of the chapter element. Like all subelements of an element, the tags of the section subelement falls within the tags of the chapter element.

✦ The text This is the first line. and This is the second line. is the textual content of this element.

✦ The tag <br/> represents a nonempty element that is a subelement of the section element.

So one set of tags, which represents an element, can contain another element, or a subelement, which in turn is denoted by a tag or set of tags.

Because one set of tags can contain another, or *nest* within another, the tags have to appear in the correct order so that the XML processor can read and process them without a problem. A set of a start-tag and a corresponding end-tag that delimits a subelement must nest within the set of a start-tag and a corresponding end-tag that marks the element containing the subelement.

Here is an example of improper nesting:

```
<chapter>
<section>
This is the first line.<br/>
This is the second line.
</chapter>
</section>
```

The XML processor would flag this as an error, because the end-tag of the `section` subelement appears outside of the end-tag of the `chapter` element. To correct this problem, simply reverse the order of the `section` and `chapter` end-tags:

```
<chapter>
<section>
This is the first line.<br/>
This is the second line.
</section>
</chapter>
```

Now the `section` tags properly nest within the `chapter` tags.

In this case, it makes logical sense that a section falls within a chapter, so the corresponding tags should nest this way. (To ensure that your document makes logical sense, you'd use a DTD that explains the logical order of `section` and `chapter` as well as a validating XML processor to make sure the document is correct.)

You may run into other situations in which the order that the elements appear doesn't matter. Such a situation is when you have to format a piece of text as both bold and italic. The DTD, if you use one, may not specify whether bold is a subelement of italic or vice versa. Even if it doesn't matter that neither element is a subelement of the other, it's still vital to nest the tags of the elements properly.

For example, this code

```
<b><i>This text is both bold and italic.</b></i>
```

would trigger an error with the XML processor because the tags are not nested correctly. To fix this problem, simply reverse either the two start-tags or the two end-tags. Both of these examples

```
<b><i>This text is both bold and italic. </i></b>
```

```
<i><b>This text is both bold and italic.</b></i>
```

would work because in both cases, the elements nest properly.

In addition, the case of the element Names must match—not only each other, but also the Names provided in their associated element declarations.

For example, this code

```
<b><i>This text is both bold and italic.</B></I>
```

would trigger an error with the XML processor because the case of the `<b>` start-tag does not match the case of the `</B>` end-tag; same with the `<i>` start-tag and the `</I>` end-tag. To fix this problem, simply change either the two start-tags or the two end-tags so that the cases match each other as well as the element Name. Either of these examples

```
<b><i>This text is both bold and italic. </i></b>
```

```
<B><I>This text is both bold and italic. </I></B>
```

could work as long as the case of these element Names matches the case of the Names in their respective element declarations.

Also, keep in mind that attributes may only appear in start-tags, including the tags of empty elements; you may not specify an attribute in an end-tag.

Part V

Physical Structures

The building blocks that make up XML are called *physical structures*. Physical structures are composed of a variety of materials, including virtual storage units of data (known as entities), single characters, files, pointers to other sources of information, and whole documents. A physical structure can be as small as a bit of data or as large as an entire application. Taken all together, individual physical structures make up the general physical structure of an XML document. It may take some time and patience to learn how to define and use physical structures, but once you understand the concepts, you can master some of the most important and robust capabilities of XML.

In this part . . .

- ✓ **Accessing the wide variety of character classes**
- ✓ **Encoding characters**
- ✓ **Referencing characters and entities**
- ✓ **Designing powerful entity and character expansions**
- ✓ **Creating a document entity**
- ✓ **Declaring a variety of entities**
- ✓ **Using the most appropriate entity for each purpose**
- ✓ **Including non-XML components in your documents by using binary entities**
- ✓ **Using parameter entities to make your DTD modular**
- ✓ **Declaring notations**

Characters and Entities

A *character* — in XML or any computer application — consists of a single base-2 (8-, 16-, or even 32-bit) chunk of data. Because of how XML organizes textual data, each character is significant in XML. Similarly, knowing how to effectively use groups or sets of characters in your documents is crucial for creating efficient and robust XML documents. Entities can identify characters, character classes, or special characters, and so you can think of entities and characters as partners in creating and organizing the single data chunks of physical structure.

Character classes

The set of characters — or *character class* — forms the basis of XML data. XML conforms to the Unicode standard and groups characters into several distinctive classes:

+ **Base characters** contain the alphabetic characters of the Latin alphabet, without diacritics. (A *diacritic* is a mark applied or attached to a character to create an entirely different character.)

+ **Ideographic characters** are graphic symbols retained by single bytes of data. Ideographic characters may represent *Han* (Asian) symbols.

+ **Combining characters** combine with or attach to the visible form of another character. Combining characters contain most of the diacritics.

+ **Digits** are characters within a range of numbers.

+ **Extenders** are symbols beyond the character sets defined previously.

The base character and ideographic classes combine to form the larger class of *letters,* which are essentially characters in any alphabet.

The general rule in the XML Specification for a letter reads like this:

```
Letter ::= BaseChar | Ideographic
```

According to this rule, `Letter` offers the option, as indicated by the logical "or" (`|`), of being either a base character (`BaseChar`) or an `Ideographic`.

The base character option, in turn, is defined by this very long rule in the XML Specification:

```
BaseChar := [#x0041-#x005A] | [#x0061-#x007A] |
   [#x00C0-#x00D6] | [#x00D8-#x00F6] | [#x00F8-
   #x00FF] | [#x0100-#x0131] | [#x0134-#x013E] |
   [#x0141-#x0148] | [#x014A-#x017E] | [#x0180-
   #x01C3] | [#x01CD-#x01F0] | [#x01F4-#x01F5] |
   [#x01FA-#x0217] | [#x0250-#x02A8] | [#x02BB-
   #x02C1] | #x0386 | [#x0388-#x038A] | #x038C |
   [#x038E-#x03A1] | [#x03A3-#x03CE] | [#x03D0-
   #x03D6] | #x03DA | #x03DC | #x03DE | #x03E0 |
   [#x03E2-#x03F3] | [#x0401-#x040C] | [#x040E-
   #x044F] | [#x0451-#x045C] | [#x045E-#x0481] |
   [#x0490-#x04C4] | [#x04C7-#x04C8] | [#x04CB-
   #x04CC] | [#x04D0-#x04EB] | [#x04EE-#x04F5] |
   [#x04F8-#x04F9] | [#x0531-#x0556] | #x0559 |
   [#x0561-#x0586] | [#x05D0-#x05EA] | [#x05F0-
   #x05F2] | [#x0621-#x063A] | [#x0641-#x064A] |
   [#x0671-#x06B7] | [#x06BA-#x06BE] | [#x06C0-
   #x06CE] | [#x06D0-#x06D3] | #x06D5 | [#x06E5-
   #x06E6] | [#x0905-#x0939] | #x093D | [#x0958-
   #x0961] | [#x0985-#x098C] | [#x098F-#x0990] |
   [#x0993-#x09A8] | [#x09AA-#x09B0] | #x09B2 |
   [#x09B6-#x09B9] | [#x09DC-#x09DD] | [#x09DF-
   #x09E1] | [#x09F0-#x09F1] | [#x0A05-#x0A0A] |
   [#x0A0F-#x0A10] | [#x0A13-#x0A28] | [#x0A2A-
   #x0A30] | [#x0A32-#x0A33] | [#x0A35-#x0A36] |
   [#x0A38-#x0A39] | [#x0A59-#x0A5C] | #x0A5E |
   [#x0A72-#x0A74] | [#x0A85-#x0A8B] | #x0A8D |
   [#x0A8F-#x0A91] | [#x0A93-#x0AA8] | [#x0AAA-
   #x0AB0] | [#x0AB2-#x0AB3] | [#x0AB5-#x0AB9] |
   #x0ABD | #x0AE0 | [#x0B05-#x0B0C] | [#x0B0F-
   #x0B10] | [#x0B13-#x0B28] | [#x0B2A-#x0B30] |
   [#x0B32-#x0B33] | [#x0B36-#x0B39] | #x0B3D |
   [#x0B5C-#x0B5D] | [#x0B5F-#x0B61] | [#x0B85-
   #x0B8A] | [#x0B8E-#x0B90] | [#x0B92-#x0B95] |
   [#x0B99-#x0B9A] | #x0B9C | [#x0B9E-#x0B9F] |
   [#x0BA3-#x0BA4] | [#x0BA8-#x0BAA] | [#x0BAE-
   #x0BB5] | [#x0BB7-#x0BB9] | [#x0C05-#x0C0C] |
   [#x0C0E-#x0C10] | [#x0C12-#x0C28] | [#x0C2A-
   #x0C33] | [#x0C35-#x0C39] | [#x0C60-#x0C61] |
   [#x0C85-#x0C8C] | [#x0C8E-#x0C90] | [#x0C92-
   #x0CA8] | [#x0CAA-#x0CB3] | [#x0CB5-#x0CB9] |
   #x0CDE | [#x0CE0-#x0CE1] | [#x0D05-#x0D0C] |
   [#x0D0E-#x0D10] | [#x0D12-#x0D28] | [#x0D2A-
   #x0D39] | [#x0D60-#x0D61] | [#x0E01-#x0E2E] |
   #x0E30 | [#x0E32-#x0E33] | [#x0E40-#x0E45] |
   [#x0E81-#x0E82] | #x0E84 | [#x0E87-#x0E88] |
   #x0E8A | #x0E8D | [#x0E94-#x0E97] | [#x0E99-
   #x0E9F] | [#x0EA1-#x0EA3] | #x0EA5 | #x0EA7 |
   [#x0EAA-#x0EAB] | [#x0EAD-#x0EAE] | #x0EB0 |
   [#x0EB2-#x0EB3] | #x0EBD | [#x0EC0-#x0EC4] |
   [#x0F40-#x0F47] | [#x0F49-#x0F69] | [#x10A0-
   #x10C5] | [#x10D0-#x10F6] | #x1100 | [#x1102-
   #x1103] | [#x1105-#x1107] | #x1109 | [#x110B-
   #x110C] | [#x110E-#x1112] | #x113C | #x113E |
   #x1140 | #x114C | #x114E | #x1150 | [#x1154-
   #x1155] | #x1159 | [#x115F-#x1161] | #x1163 |
```

(continued)

(continued)

```
#x1165 | #x1167 | #x1169 | [#x116D-#x116E] |
[#x1172-#x1173] | #x1175 | #x119E | #x11A8 |
#x11AB | [#x11AE-#x11AF] | [#x11B7-#x11B8] |
#x11BA | [#x11BC-#x11C2] | #x11EB | #x11F0 |
#x11F9 | [#x1E00-#x1E9B] | [#x1EA0-#x1EF9] |
[#x1F00-#x1F15] | [#x1F18-#x1F1D] | [#x1F20-
#x1F45] | [#x1F48-#x1F4D] | [#x1F50-#x1F57] |
#x1F59 | #x1F5B | #x1F5D | [#x1F5F-#x1F7D] |
[#x1F80-#x1FB4] | [#x1FB6-#x1FBC] | #x1FBE |
[#x1FC2-#x1FC4] | [#x1FC6-#x1FCC] | [#x1FD0-
#x1FD3] | [#x1FD6-#x1FDB] | [#x1FE0-#x1FEC] |
[#x1FF2-#x1FF4] | [#x1FF6-#x1FFC] | #x2126 |
[#x212A-#x212B] | #x212E | [#x2180-#x2182] |
[#x3041-#x3094] | [#x30A1-#x30FA] | [#x3105-
#x312C] | [#xAC00-#xD7A3]
```

Essentially, this long list shows the options between individual characters and ranges of characters that you can use in XML. The codes are hexadecimal codes that correspond to Unicode character sets.

The set of ideographic characters is comparatively simple:

```
Ideographic := [#x4E00-#x9FA5] | #x3007 | [#x3021-
#x3029]
```

The set of nonletters includes combining characters, digits, and extenders.

The XML Specification rule for combining characters (CombiningChar) indicates a fairly long set of options:

```
CombiningChar := [#x0300-#x0345] | [#x0360-#x0361]
| [#x0483-#x0486] | [#x0591-#x05A1] | [#x05A3-
#x05B9] | #x05BB#x05BD | #x05BF | [#x05C1-
#x05C2] | #x05C4 | #x064B#x0652 | #x0670 |
[#x06D6-#x06DC] | #x06DD#x06DF | [#x06E0-
#x06E4] | [#x06E7-#x06E8] | [#x06EA-#x06ED] |
[#x0901-#x0903] | #x093C | [#x093E-#x094C] |
#x094D | [#x0951-#x0954] | [#x0962-#x0963] |
[#x0981-#x0983] | #x09BC | #x09BE | #x09BF |
[#x09C0-#x09C4] | [#x09C7-#x09C8] | [#x09CB-
#x09CD] | #x09D7 | [#x09E2-#x09E3] | #x0A02 |
#x0A3C | #x0A3E | #x0A3F | [#x0A40-#x0A42] |
[#x0A47-#x0A48] | [#x0A4B-#x0A4D] | [#x0A70-
#x0A71] | [#x0A81-#x0A83] | #x0ABC | [#x0ABE-
#x0AC5] | [#x0AC7-#x0AC9] | [#x0ACB-#x0ACD] |
[#x0B01-#x0B03] | #x0B3C | [#x0B3E-#x0B43] |
[#x0B47-#x0B48] | [#x0B4B-#x0B4D] | [#x0B56-
#x0B57] | [#x0B82-#x0B83] | [#x0BBE-#x0BC2] |
[#x0BC6-#x0BC8] | [#x0BCA-#x0BCD] | #x0BD7 |
[#x0C01-#x0C03] | [#x0C3E-#x0C44] | [#x0C46-
#x0C48] | [#x0C4A-#x0C4D] | [#x0C55-#x0C56] |
[#x0C82-#x0C83] | [#x0CBE-#x0CC4] | [#x0CC6-
#x0CC8] | [#x0CCA-#x0CCD] | [#x0CD5-#x0CD6] |
```

```
[#x0D02-#x0D03] | [#x0D3E-#x0D43] | [#x0D46-
#x0D48] | [#x0D4A-#x0D4D] | #x0D57 | #x0E31 |
[#x0E34-#x0E3A] | [#x0E47-#x0E4E] | #x0EB1 |
[#x0EB4-#x0EB9] | [#x0EBB-#x0EBC] | [#x0EC8-
#x0ECD] | [#x0F18-#x0F19] | #x0F35 | #x0F37 |
#x0F39 | #x0F3E | #x0F3F | [#x0F71-#x0F84] |
[#x0F86-#x0F8B] | [#x0F90-#x0F95] | #x0F97 |
[#x0F99-#x0FAD] | [#x0FB1-#x0FB7] | #x0FB9 |
[#x20D0-#x20DC] | #x20E1 | [#x302A-#x302F] |
#x3099 | #x309A
```

Similarly, the XML Specification rule for digits 0–9 looks like this:

```
Digit := [#x0030-#x0039] | [#x0660-#x0669] |
   [#x06F0-#x06F9] | [#x0966-#x096F] | [#x09E6-
   #x09EF] | [#x0A66-#x0A6F] | [#x0AE6-#x0AEF] |
   [#x0B66-#x0B6F] | [#x0BE7-#x0BEF] | [#x0C66-
   #x0C6F] | [#x0CE6-#x0CEF] | [#x0D66-#x0D6F] |
   [#x0E50-#x0E59] | [#x0ED0-#x0ED9] | [#x0F20-
   #x0F29]
```

And finally, the XML Specification rule for extender characters:

```
Extender ::= #x00B7 | #x02D0 | #x02D1 | #x0387 |
   #x0640 | #x0E46 | #x0EC6 | #x3005 | [#x3031-
   #x3035] | [#x309D-#x309E] | [#x30FC-#x30FE]
```

If you want a detailed explanation of how to read notions from the XML Specification, check out Chapter 4 of *XML For Dummies*.

All of these rules comprise the technical specification for character classes. You probably won't want to go through each hexadecimal code or range, but if you're concerned about Unicode compatibility, you need to know the following to use the Unicode-defined character classes properly:

✦ Name-start characters, or characters that begin an XML Name, must conform to one of the categories in the Unicode database: Ll, Lu, Lo, Lt, or Nl.

✦ Name characters other than Name-start characters must conform to one of the categories Mc, Me, Mn, Lm, or Nd.

✦ You may not use characters in the compatibility area, which is in the range of character codes greater than #xF900 and less than #xFFFE, in XML Names.

✦ The characters within the range [#x02BB-#x02C1] and the individual characters #x0559, #x06E5, and #x06E6 are treated as Name-start characters rather than as Name characters, because the property file classifies them as "Alphabetic."

✦ In accordance with the Unicode Specification, Section 5.14, you may not use characters within the range [#x20DD-#x20E0].

♦ Character #x00B7 (a round bullet symbol) is classified as an extender.

♦ Character #x0387 is a Name character, because #x00B7 is its canonical equivalent.

♦ You may not use the colon (:) or underscore (_) as a Name-start character.

♦ You may use the hyphen (-) and the full stop (.) as name characters.

 Check out Chapter 9 of *XML For Dummies* for information about commonly used special characters. For more information about the Unicode set, check the Unicode Consortium home page at www.unicode.org/. For more information about characters, ***see also*** Part III.

Character encoding in entities

XML uses the Unicode (ISO 10646) standard for encoding characters in text. This standard offers a tremendous amount of flexibility within XML, because you can choose one of several methods for encoding characters as bit patterns. Such a method is called a *character encoding scheme.* The most common character encoding schemes are the 8-bit scheme, known as *UTF-8,* and the 16-bit scheme, known as *UTF-16.* Both schemes support the entire Unicode range. However, UTF-8 can be mapped only to a 255-character range at a given time. UTF-16 can support all the Unicode characters at once without having to remap, but it uses more memory overhead. (You can use a 32-bit character encoding scheme, but you may not want or really need to reference such a wide choice of characters in your document.)

 For more information about the Unicode standard, check the Unicode Consortium home page at www.unicode.org/.

You tell the XML processor which encoding scheme you need to use by using an *encoding declaration,* which is a processing instruction (PI) that is part of the XML declaration.

 The set of rules for character encoding appears like this in the XML Specification:

```
EncodingDecl ::= S 'encoding' Eq '"' EncName '"' |
    "'" EncName "'"

EncName ::= [A-Za-z] ([A-Za-z0-9._] | '-')* /
    *Encoding name contains only Latin characters*/
```

The first rule for the encoding declaration (EncodingDecl) indicates that you simply enter a white space (S), the literal string encoding, an equals sign (the character =, denoted by Eq), and the encoding Name (`EncName`) within double or single quotes (or apostrophes), respectively. Of course, you put this entire encoding declaration within the XML declaration or within an entity declaration.

The second rule for encoding Names (`EncName`) states that, in the declaration, you must use a Name consisting of only Latin alphabetic characters (`A` to `Z` and `a` to `z`), digits (`0` to `9`), full stops (`.`), hyphens (`-`), and underscores (`_`). This limitation exists so that your XML processor can read the encoding declaration itself without ambiguity before deciding how to encode the other characters.

For more information about characters and processing instructions, *see also* Part III.

An encoding declaration looks like this in the PI:

```
<?XML encoding="[EncodingDescription]" ?>
```

You may use one of the following values for the
`[EncodingDescription]`:

- ✦ Unicode/ISO/IEC 10646 encoding:
  - `UTF-8`
  - `UTF-16`
  - `ISO-10646-UCS-2`
  - `ISO-10646-UCS-4`
- ✦ ISO 8859 encoding: `ISO-8859-1` through `ISO-8859-9`
- ✦ JIS X-0208-1997 encoding:
  - `ISO-2022-JP`
  - `Shift_JIS`
  - `EUC_JP`

You must refer to miscellaneous character encodings registered with the Internet Assigned Numbers Authority (IANA) by their registered names. (The reference to IANA characters is case-insensitive.)

Here are a few examples of encoding declarations:

```
<?XML encoding="UTF-8"?>
```

```
<?XML encoding='EUC_JP'?>
```

```
<?XML encoding='ISO-10646-UCS-4'?>
```

The first example is probably the most common encoding declaration, although you don't have to use it because XML v. 1.0 processors assume UTF-8 character encoding by default.

If you declare an encoding scheme for an XML text entity, you must use the declared encoding scheme with the corresponding entity consistently throughout the document. Each text entity in an XML document may use a different encoding for its characters, however, which means you may use a combination of UTF-8 and UTF-16 (or other encoding schemes) in your documents. Combining enables you to use any alphabet within your markup. For example, you could specify that the Names of your element types use Unicode character `block U+0590-U+05FF` to produce Hebrew letters. To avoid triggering a processing error, make sure all of the characters in your text entities match the entities' encoding declarations.

When should you use the basic UTF-8 or a larger character encoding scheme? UTF-8, the smallest encoding scheme, provides you with the standard ASCII character set, which may be all you need to use within your document. You can save computer resources by adhering to the UTF-8 encoding scheme. If you regularly use characters beyond the ASCII character set, you should consider declaring your encoding with UTF-16 or another encoding scheme. UTF-16 provides you with 65,000 characters to choose from, making it a robust encoding scheme — and a very large one, because it creates files twice the byte size of UTF-8-encoded documents. You must weigh the pros and cons of each scheme before declaring the encoding. On the other hand, if you know how to mix and match encoding schemes effectively, you can use a more robust encoding scheme for certain entities that require it while maintaining the more efficient UTF-8 encoding for the rest of the document.

In addition, if you only have a smattering of non-UTF-8 characters in your document, consider using an ISO 10646 character number reference for each special character instead of declaring an encoding scheme for an entire entity.

For more information on character references, ***see also*** "Entity references" and "Character references" later in this section.

If you use UTF-16 encoding for any external entity, you must begin the entity with an appropriate encoding signature, which is the *Byte Order Mark (BOM),* a character indicated by the hexadecimal value FEFF (denoted as `#xFEFF`). The BOM is the name of a special character that tells the XML processor to byte-swap character code elements. The byte-reversed value of this character's code — in other words, its associated character if it had one — is a special code value that is not assigned to a character. The XML processor uses the BOM to differentiate between UTF-8 and UTF-16 encoded documents, and it doesn't consider this encoding signature part of either the markup or the character data of the XML document.

You can find a technical description of the Byte Order Mark in the ISO/IEC 10646 Annex E as well as in the Unicode Appendix B, indicated by the *zero width no-break space* character, #xFEFF. See the Unicode Web site at www.unicode.org/ for details.

Character references

You may need to use a character within the ISO 10646/Unicode character set that you can't enter directly via the computer keyboard or other input device. In fact, many such characters exist, and you may require some of them in your XML documents. You can include such a character in your document by using a *character reference,* which is an escape code for a single Unicode character. You do this by expressing a character reference with the numerical value of the character's bit string.

The rule for a character reference appears like this in the XML Specification:

```
CharRef ::= '&#' [0-9]+ ';' | '&#x' [0-9a-fA-F]+
    ';' [wfc: Legal Character]
```

According to this rule, you can express a character reference with either

✦ A *decimal reference,* which is

- A number consisting of digits 0 through 9.

- Preceded by an ampersand and a pound sign (&#).

- Immediately followed by a semicolon (;).

✦ A *hexadecimal reference,* which is

- A base-16 number consisting of digits 0 through 9 and/or letters A (or a) through F (or f).

- Preceded by an ampersand, pound sign, and the literal string x (&#x).

- Immediately followed by a semicolon (;).

Both types of numbers refer to specific characters in the Unicode character set.

The well-formedness constraint (wfc:), Legal Character, indicates that the characters referenced must be legal according to the character range specified by the XML Specification in the rule char.

You denote the standard Rx prescription symbol (℞) — represented by the Unicode character number U+211E — by the decimal reference ℞ and by the hexadecimal reference ℞. Although you couldn't tell just by looking at them, both of these numeric values refer to the same Unicode symbol.

Similarly, you denote the copyright symbol (©) by both the decimal reference © and the hexadecimal reference ©.

Here is an example of how a character reference may appear in a document:

```
Press the <key>less-than</key> key (&#x3C;) to
    invoke the macro.
```

Check out Chapter 9 of *XML For Dummies* to get an extensive list of special characters. For more information about the XML Specification, ***see also*** Part II. To find out more about the Unicode set, check the Unicode Consortium home page at `www.unicode.org/`. For more information about characters, ***see also*** Part III.

Entity references

An *entity reference* is a pointer — or an alias — to the content of a named entity. You may specify references for two types of entities:

✦ **General entities,** whose references use the ampersand (&) and the semicolon (;) as beginning- and end-delimiters, respectively.

✦ **Parameter entities,** whose references use the percent sign (%) and semicolon (;) as beginning- and end-delimiters, respectively.

The rule that defines a reference appears like this in the XML Specification:

```
Reference ::= EntityRef | CharRef
```

This rule is quite simple: It says that a reference can be either an entity reference (EntityRef) or a character reference (CharRef), because the logical "or" (|) divides the two types of references.

The two rules immediately following this one define the syntax of an entity reference and of a parameter entity reference (PEReference).

Here is the rule for an entity reference:

```
EntityRef ::= '&' Name ';'
[wfc: Entity Declared]
[vc: Entity Declared]
[wfc: Parsed Entity]
[wfc: No Recursion]
```

This rule contains three well-formedness checks and one validity check.

First, the well-formedness constraint (wfc:), Entity Declared, indicates that the Name given in the entity reference must match the Name provided in the entity declaration in the following cases:

+ In a DTD-less document

+ In a document that only has an internal DTD subset and that doesn't contain any parameter entity references

+ In a document with a standalone document declaration of "yes" (standalone='yes')

In addition, this constraint requires that you declare a parameter entity before referencing it. Similarly, you must declare a general entity before referencing it when it appears in a default value in an attribute-list declaration.

The exception to this constraint is that you don't have to declare any of these entities:

+ amp (&)

+ lt (<)

+ gt (>)

+ apos (')

+ quot (")

The XML processor automatically recognizes the corresponding entity references for these special entities. This is useful to, say, differentiate between a less-than symbol (<) in the textual content of your document and the delimiter that marks the beginning of markup.

If you enter an ampersand (&) directly into the string Bonnie & Clyde, Inc. within the textual content of your document, the XML processor signals an error. The way to correct this is to use the amp entity, which inserts a literal ampersand into the document:

```
Bonnie &amp; Clyde, Inc.                    .
```

Second, the validity constraint (vc:), Entity Declared, indicates that in a document with an external subset or external parameter entities with a standalone document declaration of "no" (standalone='no'), you must make sure the Name in the entity reference matches the Name you declared for the entity. And like the well-formedness constraint of Entity Declared, you must declare a parameter entity before referencing it; similarly, you must declare a general entity before referencing it when it appears in a default value in an attribute-list declaration.

Third, the well-formedness constraint, `Parsed Entity`, means that an entity reference must not contain the Name of an unparsed entity, also known as a binary entity. You may only refer to unparsed or binary entities in attribute values that are declared of type `ENTITY` (or `ENTITIES`).

Finally, the well-formedness constraint, `No Recursion`, tells you that a parsed entity must not contain a recursive reference to itself, either directly or indirectly.

Consider the following entity:

```
<!ENTITY XML "Extensible Markup Language">
```

A legal reference for this entity would be `&XML;`. If you could somehow insert another reference to the `XML` entity within the `&XML;` reference, the processor would keep inserting `Extensible Markup Language` forever.

Here is an example of two entity references that point to the entities `docdate` and `security-level` respectively:

```
On &docdate;, you will be given &security-level;
    security clearance.
```

For more information on entities, ***see also*** the "Entities" section later in this part.

Here is the rule for a parameter entity reference:

```
PEReference ::= '%' Name ';'
[wfc: Entity Declared]
[vc: Entity Declared]
[wfc: Parsed Entity]
[wfc: No Recursion]
[wfc: In DTD]
```

This rule contains four well-formedness checks and one validity check. The first four checks are the same as the ones in the rule for the entity reference. The last check, the well-formedness constraint, `In DTD`, specifies that parameter entity references may only appear in a DTD. Because parameter entities and parameter entity references can only appear in a DTD, entity references and character references are the types of references that you would see throughout an XML document.

An entity declaration for a URL looks like this:

```
<!ENTITY % ISOLat2 SYSTEM "http://www.xml.com/iso/
    isolat2-xml.entities">
```

The parameter entity reference, as configured by this declaration, looks like this:

```
%ISOLat2;
```

To find more information on parameter entities, ***see also*** the "Parameter entities" subsection of the "Entities" section later in this part.

Expansion of entity and character references

Your document can get rather complicated when you use entity and character references extensively. The XML processor recognizes and *expands* — that is, it parses and resolves — entity and character references in a predetermined sequence. To avoid triggering processor errors or creating differences from what you had intended for your document, you need to keep track of all your references and know what each one does.

Consider this declaration in a DTD:

```
<!ENTITY ampersand "<p>You may escape an ampersand
  (&#38;#38;) with the numeric value
  &#38;#38;#38; or by using the general entity
  &amp;amp;.</p>" >
```

This looks pretty complicated, but if you follow the logic, you can understand what's going on.

The XML processor recognizes the character references as it parses this entity declaration, and it resolves them before doing anything else. After the processor resolves these references, it stores the following string as the value of the entity `ampersand`:

```
<p>You may escape an ampersand (&#38;) with the
  numeric value &#38;#38; or by using the general
  entity &amp;amp;.</p>
```

When the processor detects a reference to `&ampersand;` in the document, it reparses the text. Then the processor recognizes the start- and end-tags of the paragraph (p) element, and also recognizes and expands the three references (`&#38;`, `&#38;#38;`, and `&amp;amp;`).

This entire process creates a `p` element with this content:

```
You may escape an ampersand (&) with the numeric
  value &#38; or by using the general entity
  &amp;.
```

This line of text, by the way, consists of only data, but no delimiters or markup, because it's the result of what the processor parsed.

This example illustrates how tricky using entity and character references can get. The lesson: Be careful, plan your use of references ahead of time, and keep track of what reference will expand into what entity or character.

This even more complex example demonstrates how references expand:

```
1 <?xml version='1.0'?>
2 <!DOCTYPE example [
3 <!ELEMENT example (#PCDATA) >
4 <!ENTITY % a '&#38;b;'>
5 <!ENTITY % b '&#60;!ENTITY clumsy "difficult to
    follow" >' >
6 %a;
7 ]>
8 <example>This example demonstrates an XML method
    that is legal but &clumsy;.</example>
```

Normally, you don't have line numbers prefacing each line in an XML document, as in this example. I added the line numbers so that you can more easily follow the logic of the explanation below.

You can determine the result of this example by understanding how the processor expands each reference and by putting the expanded text together:

+ First, in Line 4, the processor immediately expands the character reference `&#38;` which is the escape-character sequence representing the ampersand (&), and stores the parameter entity a in the symbol table with the value `%b;`.

+ The processor doesn't rescan the replacement text at this time, and so it doesn't recognize the reference to parameter entity b. (Even if the processor did recognize parameter entity b, it would trigger an error because b is not yet declared.)

+ In Line 5, the processor immediately expands the character reference `&#60;`, which is the escape-character sequence representing the left-angle bracket (<), and stores the parameter entity b with the replacement text `<!ENTITY clumsy "difficult to follow" >`, which is a well-formed entity declaration.

+ In Line 6, the processor recognizes the reference to a and parses the replacement text of a, which is `%b;`. In turn, the processor recognizes the reference to b and parses its replacement text (`<!ENTITY clumsy "difficult to follow" >`). The general entity clumsy is now declared with the replacement text `difficult to follow`.

+ Finally, in Line 8, the processor recognizes the reference to the general entity clumsy and expands it.

Now, the full textual content of the `example` element is the string:

```
This example demonstrates an XML method that is
    legal but difficult to follow.
```

This example is a bit ridiculous, but by analyzing it you can understand why you need to keep track of how you use entity and character references.

 For more information about characters within the Unicode standard, check the Unicode Consortium home page at `www.unicode.org/`.

Entities

You can break an XML document into one or more units, each of which contains data. Such virtual storage units of data are called *entities*. An entity is the essential building block of physical structure in XML. In fact, the reason physical structure is *physical* is that the data referred to by entities is physically located somewhere, such as in a file on a disk drive or in a field of a database.

Each entity consists of

✦ A *name,* which identifies the entity.

✦ A *value,* which is sometimes called the *content* of the entity. The value is either the data of the entity itself or it is a pointer to the data.

Each entity's name is mapped to its corresponding value or content. You can use entities to retrieve anything from a single character to a large file.

Each XML document has one essential entity called the *document entity* or the *root entity,* which serves as the starting point for the XML processor and which may contain the entire document.

To find more information on the document entity, ***see also*** "Document entity" later in this section.

Entities fall into two general classifications:

✦ Parsed and unparsed entities

✦ Internal and external entities

Both parsed and unparsed entities may be either internal or external entities.

For more information on parsed and unparsed entities, ***see also*** "Parsed and unparsed entities" later in this section.

In addition, here is another classification of parsed entities:

✦ Parsed entities used within the document content are called *general entities*. You reference general entities by the name of the entity beginning with an ampersand (&) and ending with a semicolon (;).

✦ *Parameter entities* are parsed entities used only within the DTD. You reference parameter entities by the name of the entity beginning with a percent sign (%) and ending with a semicolon (;).

General and parameter entities use different forms of reference and have different purposes.

You can find more information on general entities in "External entities" and "Internal entities" later in this section. For more on parameter entities, *see also* "Parameter entities" later in this section.

You can use any of the entities that fall into the aforementioned classifications to refer to repeated or varying text and to include the content of external files.

The last classification of entities is predefined entities, which you use to represent special characters.

You can find more information on special characters in Part III. For more on predefined entities, *see also* "Predefined entities" later in this section.

Document entity

All entities, no matter how large or small, are units of data. Some entities contain smaller entities. The largest entity, or the entity that contains all other entities, is the *document entity*.

If you created an outline of all the entities in your document, you may find that some entities contain smaller entities that contain still smaller entities. The largest entities in this case are like the branches of a tree, which yield smaller branches, and even smaller branches off those. The trunk of the tree is the starting point for all the branches. In XML, the tree trunk of a document — the document entity, which is also known as the *root* — serves as the starting point (as well as the ending point, if you will) for an XML processor. For this reason, the document entity is the first text entity you encounter when reading an XML document.

If you use entities to divide a large document into sections, you can use a document entity, in a separate file, to efficiently organize the sections.

Say you have a screenplay with three acts: act1, act2, and act3. Each act is a unit of data, or an entity. You could set up entity references for each of the acts and refer to them within the root element of the screenplay (screenplay) like this:

```
<screenplay>
<characterlist>[list of characters]</characterlist>
<notes>[notes]</notes>
&act1;
&act2;
&act3;
</screenplay>
```

This method works quite well, and it presents a very clean way to organize the screenplay. But watch out for this: The embedded screenplay acts can only contain markup. In other words, an act file can't have its own document type declaration (<!DOCTYPE):

```
<act>
<scene>
<setting>
The fog rolls in as MR.WATSON turns to SHERLOCK
    HOLMES.
</setting>
[...]
</scene>
</act>
```

Because using this method doesn't allow the presence of a document type declaration, you can't treat each act as a complete XML document. The way to circumvent this problem is to create a separate file whose only purpose is to serve as the document entity for a single act:

```
<?XML version="1.0"?>
<!DOCTYPE act SYSTEM "screenplay.dtd" [
<!ENTITY act1 SYSTEM "act1.xml">
]>
&act1;
```

This method adds only a little overhead to your overall document scheme, but you may find the flexibility of each act being its own well-formed document worthwhile.

The document entity is well-formed if it matches the Name in the document type declaration, which is also the element type of the root element.

This document isn't well-formed:

```
<?XML version="1.0"?>
<!DOCTYPE note SYSTEM "note.dtd">
<memo>This document isn't well-formed, because the
    root element "memo" does not match the DOCTYPE
    "note".</memo>
```

A simple modification makes this document well-formed:

```
<?XML version="1.0"?>
<!DOCTYPE note SYSTEM "note.dtd">
<note>Now everything matches, so this document
    won't trigger an error.</note>
```

Changing the DOCTYPE to memo and keeping the memo root element would have worked just as well.

For more information about the XML Specification, *see also* Part II. To find out more about well-formedness and document type declarations, *see also* Part III. For more about root elements, *see also* Part IV. You can find more information on entity references in the "Entity references" and "Character references" subsections of the "Characters and Entities" section earlier in this part.

Entity declarations

An *entity declaration* defines the name of an entity and associates it with a corresponding replacement string or with data that is stored externally and identified by a URL. Like all other types of declarations, an entity declaration is located within the DTD.

You can use an entity declaration to associate a Name with another fragment of the document, such as

+ A string of regular text

+ A section of the document type declaration

+ A reference to an external file that contains either

  • XML text

  • Binary data

The set of rules for entity declarations appears like this in the XML Specification:

```
EntityDecl ::=      GEDecl /* General entities */
   | PEDecl /* Parameter entities */
GEDecl ::= '<!ENTITY' S Name S EntityDef S? '>'

PEDecl ::= '<!ENTITY' S '%' S Name S PEDef S? '>'
   /* Parameter entities */

EntityDef ::= EntityValue | ExternalDef

PEDef ::= EntityValue | ExternalID
```

The first rule in this set determines that an entity declaration (EntityDecl) can be a declaration for either a general entity (GEDecl) or a parameter entity (PEDecl). The next two rules define declarations for a general entity and a parameter entity, respectively. The final two rules describe an important piece of declarations — definitions — for both an entity and a parameter entity, respectively.

For more information about the XML Specification, check out Chapter 4 of *XML For Dummies,* or ***see also*** Part II of this book. You can find more on general entities in "External entities" and "Internal entities" later in this section. You can also find more information on parameter entities in "Parameter entities" later in this section.

If you declare the same entity more than once, the XML processor accepts only the first declaration it encounters. Some processors issue a warning if you declare the same entities multiple times.

Here are some examples of entity declarations:

```
<!ENTITY XFDQR "XML For Dummies Quick Reference">
```

This declaration is for a simple internal entity, in which the entity Name XFDQR is associated with the text string XML For Dummies Quick Reference.

```
<!ENTITY formletter SYSTEM "/standards/
    formletter.xml">
```

This declaration is for an external entity named formletter, which refers to the XML file formletter.xml in the local /standards/ directory.

```
<!ENTITY logo SYSTEM "/graphics/logo.bmp" NDATA
    BMP>
```

This declaration is also for an external entity, but the name logo is associated with a file containing binary data (/graphics/ logo.bmp) rather than XML text data. The notation BMP for a bitmap file must be declared in a separate notation declaration; the purpose of NDATA is to let the processor know to look for an accompanying notation declaration.

```
<!ENTITY % table SYSTEM "table1.xml">
```

This declaration looks just like a declaration for an external entity, one that associates the Name table with the local file table1.xml. The only difference is that this declaration contains a percent sign (%), which indicates that table is the Name of a parameter entity, and must therefore only be used within a DTD.

```
<!ENTITY % list " UL | OL | LI ">
```

Another parameter entity, the Name list is associated with a set of options or components: UL for an unordered list, OL for an ordered list, and LI for a line item. You must declare each of these options somewhere in the DTD for the XML processor to recognize them.

You can find more information on external entities in "External entities" later in this section. For more on internal entities, *see also* "Internal entities" later in this section. You can also find more information on parameter entities in "Parameter entities" later in this section.

Entity processing

The XML processor doesn't treat all physical structures in the same way. In fact, document entities, text entities, binary entities, character references, general entity references, predefined entities, and parameter entities are each processed in a unique way. This section describes the restrictions and unique processing treatment of each type of physical structure.

The XML application that you use determines how the XML processor locates the document entity. Generally, you don't need to be concerned with this, as long as you've incorporated into your document a single document entity that conforms to the rules of XML.

Of course, with nondocument entities, you may declare more than one, as long as you avoid declaring the same entity more than once. The XML processor may issue a warning or trigger an error if you declare the same entity more than once.

With external entities, providing an accurate and valid URL with the SYSTEM or PUBLIC identifier is important. If you declare an entity with a PUBLIC identifier, the XML processor may attempt to use that identifier to generate a URL for the declared entity. If the processor can't generate a URL, it uses the SYSTEM identifier that accompanies the PUBLIC identifier. The processor follows this routine to provide the application with an actual entity when possible; keep in mind, however, that you must provide at least one valid URL (either for the SYSTEM or the PUBLIC identifier) for the processor to do this.

The XML processor treats character and general entity references according to these rules:

✦ It informs the XML application of the presence of the entity reference and provides its name or number.

  • In the case of external entities, it provides the SYSTEM and PUBLIC identifiers.

  • In the case of binary external entities, it provides the notation name and its related data.

✦ When it passes a stream of textual data to the application, it removes the reference itself from that stream.

✦ In a related process, it replaces character references and internal entities with its character or textual data.

✦ Similarly, it interprets any markup within that text, except when the entity itself escapes markup characters.

✦ A validating processor inserts the content of an external text entity into the document. This rule is optional in nonvalidating processors. (In fact, the advantage of using a nonvalidating processor in this case is so that you have the option of saving time and system resources by essentially ignoring the content of an external text entity.)

The XML processor resolves, or expands, parameter-entity references and character references immediately. This expansion is not the case with general-entity references, because the processor first parses the replacement text for general entities, and then it resolves the reference.

Nonvalidating XML processors automatically recognize the five predefined entities that specify the special characters used in markup delimiters (amp (&), lt (<), gt (>), apos ('), and quot (")), whether you declared them. If you use a validating processor, you must declare these entities before you reference them, anyway.

For example, the string BR&E; expands to BR&E; and the processor doesn't recognize the remaining ampersand (&) as an entity-reference delimiter.

For more information about special characters and valid XML, see Chapter 9 of *XML For Dummies,* and **see also** Part III of this book. You can find more information on predefined entities in "Predefined entities" later in this section.

This table displays how the XML processor treats, and what it requires of, character references, entity references, and unparsed entities.

	Entity Type				
	Parameter	**Internal General**	**External Parsed General**	**Unparsed**	**Character**
Reference in Content	Not recognized	Included	Included if validating	Forbidden	Included
Reference in Attribute Value	Not recognized	Included in literal	Forbidden	Forbidden	Included
Occurs as Attribute Value	Not recognized	Forbidden	Forbidden	Notify	Not recognized

(continued)

	Parameter	Internal General	External Parsed General	Unparsed	Character
Reference in Entity Value	Included in literal	Bypassed	Bypassed	Forbidden	Included
Reference in DTD	Included as PE	Forbidden	Forbidden	Forbidden	Forbidden

The labels in the left-hand column denote the contexts in which the processor recognizes the physical structures:

+ **Reference in Content:** Refers to a physical structure occurring after the start-tag and before the end-tag of an element.

+ **Reference in Attribute Value:** Means within either the value of an attribute in a start-tag or the default value in an attribute declaration.

+ **Occurs as Attribute Value:** Means that it occurs as a single Name (as opposed to a reference) that appears either as the value of an attribute that had been declared as type ENTITY, or as one of the space-separated tokens in the value of an attribute that had been declared as type ENTITIES.

+ **Reference in Entity Value:** Is a reference within the literal entity value of a parameter or an internal entity declaration.

+ **Reference in DTD:** Is a reference within either the internal or external subsets of the DTD, but outside the value of an entity or attribute declaration.

Each table field contains one of the following descriptions:

+ **Not Recognized:** The processor does not recognize the structure in any meaningful way. For example, since the percent sign (%) character has no particular significance outside the DTD, the XML processor doesn't recognize parameter entity references as markup in content. Similarly, the processor doesn't recognize the names of unparsed entities except when they appear in the value of an appropriately declared attribute.

+ **Included:** The processor includes an entity when it retrieves and processes its replacement text, as though the replacement text were an original part of the document. The replacement text may contain both character data and (except for parameter entities) markup.

+ **Included If Validating:** To validate the document, the processor recognizes a reference to a parsed entity and includes its replacement text. This is an optional feature for external entities and nonvalidating processors, so that you can choose to view a visual indication of the entity's presence and retrieve it for display.

✦ **Forbidden:** This is a fatal error, which stops the processor from continuing to process the document normally. The following occurrences trigger a fatal error:

- The presence of a reference to an unparsed entity

- The presence of any character or general-entity reference in the DTD except within the value of an entity or attribute declaration

- A reference to an external entity in an attribute value

✦ **Included in Literal:** When an entity reference appears in an attribute value, or a parameter-entity reference appears in a literal entity value, the processor expands the reference immediately. One exception is that the processor always treats a single- or double-quote character (' or ", respectively) in the replacement text as a normal data character instead of as the delimiter of a literal.

✦ **Notify:** When the name of an unparsed entity appears as a token in the value of an attribute of declared type ENTITY or ENTITIES, a validating processor informs the application of the SYSTEM and PUBLIC (if any) identifiers for both the entity and its associated notation.

✦ **Bypassed:** When a general-entity reference appears in the value of an entity declaration, the processor bypasses — essentially, ignores — the reference.

✦ **Included as PE:** When the processor recognizes and includes a parameter-entity (PE) reference in the DTD, it enlarges the entity's replacement text by attaching a single leading space character (hexadecimal code #x20) and a single trailing space character. This is so that the replacement text of parameter entities contains an integral number of grammatical tokens in the DTD.

A well-formed set of entities looks like this, according to the rule for Included in Literal:

```
<!ENTITY % C '"Correct"' >
<!ENTITY Answer "The answer is &C;" >
```

In this example, the value of the entity Answer is properly delimited by double quotes at the beginning and at the end. The fact that the replacement text of the parameter entity C itself contains two sets of quotes doesn't matter. Answer simply expands to the value The answer is '"Correct"'.

By contrast, this set of entities isn't well-formed:

```
<!ENTITY EndAttr "27'" >
<element attribute='a-&EndAttr;>
```

Here, I tried to substitute the text 27' into the value of the element, so that when it expands, it would read as 'a-27'. This substitution doesn't work, however, because the value of the element must be properly delimited by quotes both at the beginning and at the end of the value. The processor triggers an error in this case before it has a chance to expand the EndAttr entity.

For more information about DTDs and well-formedness, see Chapter 5 of *XML For Dummies,* and ***see also*** Part III. You can find more on expansion of entity and character references in the "Expansion of entity and character references" subsection of the "Characters and Entities" section earlier in this part.

External entities

An *external entity* is an entity whose declaration doesn't contain the replacement data of the entity. Or, put another way, an external entity is mapped to data located outside its declaration.

You declare an external entity by associating its name with a *SYSTEM* or *PUBLIC identifier*. This identifier provides the XML processor with the *Uniform Resource Locator (URL)* to find the file containing the entity's data:

+ The URL may point to a file found within your local disk drive or network drive; in this case, you identify the URL with the keyword SYSTEM.

+ If the URL points to a public-domain file located in a publicly accessible place, you would identify the location and filename with the keyword PUBLIC.

An entity is either internal or external, so if the entity is not internal, you must declare it as a proper external entity.

To find more information on internal entities, ***see also*** "Internal entities" later in this section.

The set of rules for an external entity appears like this in the XML Specification:

```
ExternalID ::= 'SYSTEM' S SystemLiteral | 'PUBLIC'
    S PubidLiteral S SystemLiteral

NDataDecl ::= S 'NDATA' S Name [vc: Notation
    Declared]
```

✦ The first rule simply states that you must either include a SYSTEM or a PUBLIC identifier with an appropriate literal string for either the system or the public URL, respectively.

✦ The second rule states that the presence of a notation declaration (NDataDecl) determines that the entity is unparsed (binary); otherwise, it's a parsed (text) entity. The validity constraint (vc:) Notation Declared indicates that the Name, or the type of the unparsed entity, must match the declared name of a notation.

For more information about the XML Specification, ***see also*** Part III. You can find more on parsed (text) and unparsed (binary) entities in "Parsed and unparsed entities" later in this section. You can also find detailed information about Notation Declarations in the section called "Notations and Notation Declarations" later in this part.

Here are some examples of external entity declarations:

```
<!ENTITY chapter1 SYSTEM "chapter1.xml">
```

This entity declaration maps chapter1 to the file chapter1.xml. This file is found locally (so locally, in fact, that it doesn't even require a path before the filename!), and so it's identified with the keyword SYSTEM.

```
<!ENTITY systemfile SYSTEM "http://www.dummies.com/
    systemfile.xml">
```

This entity is very similar to the one in the first example; the only difference is that the SYSTEM identifier contains an entire URL and not just a filename.

```
<!ENTITY open-hatch PUBLIC "-//Textuality//TEXT
    Standard open-hatch boilerplate//EN" "http://
    www.textuality.com/boilerplate/OpenHatch.xml">
```

With the keyword PUBLIC, you can tell that this entity is mapped to an externally-located file.

```
<!ENTITY image SYSTEM "../graphics/image.gif" NDATA
    GIF>
```

The value of this entity is found locally, but it's not mapped to textual data. This unparsed, or binary, entity is associated with a GIF graphic image file. It's appropriately marked with NDATA, indicating that a notation declaration for GIF exists somewhere within the DTD.

Generally, external entities are unique to particular documents, and so you might want to declare them within the internal DTD subset rather than in a class DTD.

Internal entities

An *internal entity* has a value that's included literally within its entity declaration. Or, put another way, an internal entity provides both the name of the entity and the data that the entity is mapped to in one convenient package.

Because including binary data within an internal entity declaration is impossible (or at least terribly inconvenient), all internal entities are parsed, or composed of textual data. The textual data that is mapped to an internal entity is always delimited by quotes.

A declaration for an internal entity looks like this:

```
<!ENTITY Name "Textual data">
```

The quotes could also be single quotes, or apostrophes:

```
<!ENTITY Name 'Textual data'>
```

For more information about literals, *see also* Part II. To find out more about declarations, *see also* Part III. You can find more information on character references in the "Entity references" and "Character references" subsections of the "Characters and Entities" section earlier in this part. You can also find detailed information about parameter entities in "Parameter entities" later in this section.

Here are some examples of internal entity declarations:

```
<!ENTITY straightforward "This is straightforward
    replacement text for a general entity">
```

In this case, the entity straightforward is simply replaced by the literal string This is straightforward replacement text for a general entity.

```
<!ENTITY rights "All rights reserved">
```

This more useful example is of an internal general entity. Whenever the author includes the entity reference &rights;, the XML processor automatically replaces it with the literal string All rights reserved.

```
<!ENTITY % first "First Edition">
```

This declaration is for an internal parameter entity. Remember, you can only use the parameter-entity reference %first; within the DTD.

```
<!ENTITY book "XML For Dummies Quick Reference:
    Mariva H. Aviram, &#xA9; 1998 %first;,
    &rights;">
```

This declaration for an internal entity is a bit complex. You can expand it manually one step at a time:

✦ The entity `book` uses the entity reference `&book;`. The value of `book` is everything inside the quotes, `XML For Dummies Quick Reference: Mariva H. Aviram, &#xA9; 1998 %first;, &rights;`.

✦ The XML processor expands the character reference `&#xA9;` into its associated character, ©.

✦ The processor also expands the parameter-entity reference `%first;` into the string found in the example just above this one: `First Edition`.

✦ Similarly, the processor expands the reference `&rights;` into the literal string `All rights reserved`.

✦ Putting it all together, you have `XML For Dummies Quick Reference: Mariva H. Aviram, © 1998 First Edition, All rights reserved`.

You can also include markup within the value of your internal entity:

```
<!ENTITY part5 "Part 5, <H1>Physical Structures
    </H1>">
```

This entity maps the string `Part 5, <H1>Physical Structures</H1>` — both text and markup — to the name `part5`.

As you may guess from looking at these examples, internal entities can be very useful. Just a few uses of internal entities include

✦ Defining shortcuts for frequently-typed text.

✦ Defining abbreviations for text that is expected to change, such as the edition of a book or the revision status of a document.

✦ Referring to other internal entities.

The XML processor triggers an error if you refer to internal entities recursively; that is, if the value of an internal entity contains a reference to itself. Such an error protects the XML application from replacing an entity reference with the same text over and over again forever.

Parameter entities

A *parameter entity* is a text entity that's used and located only within a DTD. Besides being constrained to the DTD, a parameter entity functions just like a general entity.

For the XML processor to distinguish between a parameter entity and a general entity, you declare a parameter entity with a percent sign (%) and use the percent sign in its references instead of the ampersand (&) used in general-entity references.

You must include white space on either side of the % in the parameter-entity declaration to set it apart from the other components of the declaration. When you denote a parameter-entity reference, however, you must not allow any white space (or any other characters) in between the % and the Name of the entity.

The syntax for a parameter-entity declaration looks like this:

```
<!ENTITY % Name "Value">
```

In this syntax, Value replaces any occurrence of %Name;, which is the parameter-entity reference for Name.

The XML processor immediately expands parameter-entity references so that their replacement text can be used in other parts of the DTD.

For example:

```
<!ENTITY % version "3.2">

<!ATTLIST document version CDATA #FIXED
   "%version;">
```

In the second declaration, the declaration for the element document's attribute version, the parameter-entity reference %version; is expanded into the literal string 3.2, which was determined by the entity declaration for the parameter entity version.

Check out Chapter 5 of *XML For Dummies* to get more details about DTDs and structuring XML documents. For more information about DTDs, declarations, and white space, *see also* Part III in this book. You can find more on general entities in "External entities" and "Internal entities" earlier in this section.

Parameter entities are useful in grouping together similar types of elements in your DTD.

For example, if an element list contains several subelements:

✦ ul (unordered list)

✦ ol (ordered list)

✦ li (line item)

✦ lh (list header)

Then you can create a single parameter entity `list` that can refer to any of these list types:

```
<!ENTITY % list "ul|ol|li|lh">
```

You can then refer to this parameter entity within an element declaration for `body`:

```
<!ELEMENT body (subject|%list;|comments)*>
```

The XML processor expands the components of `body` to include:

+ `subject`
+ `ul`
+ `ol`
+ `li`
+ `lh`
+ `comments`

The result would be the same if the declaration for the element `body` looked like this:

```
<!ELEMENT body (subject|ul|ol|li|lh|comments)*>
```

But the former method divides the DTD into convenient, modular chunks and provides more clarity to human readers.

For more information about elements, ***see also*** Part IV.

You can also use a parameter entity to control the processing of conditional sections. Conditional sections use the keyword `INCLUDE` or `IGNORE` to tell the XML processor whether it should process or bypass the data within the section. If you place a parameter-entity reference where the keyword `INCLUDE` or `IGNORE` would normally occur, you can create some interesting user-controlled dynamics.

Consider the following generic conditional section in which the parameter-entity reference `%user_option;` is in the place of the INCLUDE/IGNORE switch:

```
<![%user_option;[
conditionally included declarations
]]>
```

If the parameter entity `user_option` is mapped to the value `INCLUDE`, the declarations in this conditional section are included as part of the DTD. Otherwise, the processor ignores the declarations.

In the following DTD subset:

```
<!DOCTYPE document system "document.xml" [
<!ENTITY % introduction "INCLUDE">
]>
```

Any conditional section marked by the parameter-entity reference
`%introduction;` is automatically included in the DTD. If you
change your mind about including the conditional section, simply
change the value from `INCLUDE` to `IGNORE` in the `introduction`
entity declaration.

For more information about conditional sections, *see also* Part III.

Parsed and unparsed entities

An external entity may contain one of two types of data:

 ✦ *Parsed* or *text*. Parsed data consists of XML-readable character
   data. Parsed data contains the textual content or markup that
   forms part of an XML document.

 ✦ *Unparsed* or *binary*. Unparsed data consists of code that is not
   XML-encoded. Unparsed data translates into nontext data,
   such as a graphic image, a sound file, an application, or even a
   non-XML plain-text file.

Text entities are called *parsed entities,* because the XML processor
parses all XML text. The content of a parsed entity is referred to
as its *replacement text;* this text is an integral part of the XML
document.

Conversely, the processor can't parse binary data, so *binary
entities* are called *unparsed entities*. The content of an unparsed
entity may or may not be text; even if it is text, it may not be XML-
encoded text.

The XML processor expands text-entity references immediately. In
this example

```
<!ENTITY XML "Extensible Markup Language">
```

the processor replaces the entity reference `&XML;` with the text
string `Extensible Markup Language`. So this markup

```
<p>This is an example of &XML;.</p>
```

represents the same data as

```
<p>This is an example of Extensible Markup
    Language.</p>
```

To discern a binary entity, the processor requires the presence of four items:

+ A SYSTEM identifier, which is associated with:

+ The Uniform Resource Locator (URL), indicating where the binary file is located.

+ The literal string NDATA.

+ The notation associated with the binary entity; that is, the type of binary file it is, denoted by the notation's Name, which is itself declared in an associated notation declaration.

The syntax for a binary entity looks like this:

```
<!ENTITY EntityName [SYSTEM "URL" | PUBLIC "URL"]
   NDATA NotationName>
```

Here is an example of a typical binary entity:

```
<!ENTITY logo SYSTEM "graphics/logo.bmp" NDATA BMP>
```

The entity reference &logo; refers to the binary entity logo, as declared above. The file logo is found at the URL graphics/logo.bmp. The notation BMP indicates that this file is a bitmap file; of course, the DTD must contain a notation declaration for BMP in order for this entity to be valid.

For more information about character data and markup, *see also* Part III. You can find more on entity expansion in the "Expansion of entity and character references" subsection of the "Characters and Entities" section earlier in this part. You can also find detailed information about notations and notation declarations in "Notations and Notation Declarations" later in this part.

Predefined entities

Five particular characters in XML markup need special treatment when you use them in XML text. To use any of these special characters without confusing the XML processor, you must first *escape* them with special codes. These codes are automatically recognized in XML; for this reason, they're called *predefined entities*.

The five special characters escaped by predefined entities include

+ **The ampersand:** &, escaped by the predefined entity amp.

+ **The less-than sign (or left-angle bracket):** <, escaped by the predefined entity lt.

+ **The greater-than sign (or right-angle bracket):** >, escaped by the predefined entity gt.

+ **The apostrophe (or single quote):** ', escaped by the predefined entity apos.

+ **The quotation mark (or double quote):** ", escaped by the
predefined entity quot.

You may also use numeric character references to escape these
special characters.

```
<!ENTITY amp "&#38;#38;">
```

```
<!ENTITY lt "&#38;#60;">
```

```
<!ENTITY gt "&#62;">
```

```
<!ENTITY apos "&#39;">
```

```
<!ENTITY quot "&#34;">
```

Note that the < and & characters in the declarations of lt and amp
are doubly escaped so that entity replacement is well-formed.

When the XML processor recognizes these numeric character
references, it expands them immediately and treats them as
character data.

All XML processors recognize these predefined entities whether or
not you declare them in the DTD. If you want to produce a valid
XML document, however, you must declare these entities with the
appropriate single-character values before referencing them in
your document.

For more information about special characters, markup, DTDs,
well-formedness, and validity, check out Parts I and II of *XML For
Dummies,* and ***see also*** Part III of this book. You can find more on
entity expansion in the "Expansion of entity and character references" subsection of the "Characters and Entities" section earlier
in this part.

Notations and Notation Declarations

An external binary entity is stored in a particular type of file
format. In XML, this format is known as the *notation* of the entity. A
notation could indicate any legitimate file format, such as a BMP
image, MPEG video, TXT plain-text file, or PL Perl script.

As you might expect, you declare a notation within a DTD subset
with a *notation declaration*. A notation declaration identifies a
specific type of external binary data to the XML processor so that
you can reference the data type in your document.

After the notation declaration goes to the XML application, the application does what it's programmed to do with the data type, such as spawn an image-viewer or a video player. An application that is spawned from the XML application this way is called a *helper application*. The name of the notation — which becomes its external identifier — helps the XML processor or application locate a helper application that is capable of processing the data described by the notation.

The set of three rules in the XML Specification for a notation declaration looks like this:

```
NotationDecl ::= '<!NOTATION' S Name S (ExternalID
    | PublicID) S? '>'

ExternalID ::= 'SYSTEM' S SystemLiteral | 'PUBLIC'
    S PubidLiteral S SystemLiteral

PublicID ::= 'PUBLIC' S PubidLiteral
```

The rule for the notation declaration, NotationDecl, indicates that the literal string <!NOTATION must be followed by a white space (S), which is then followed by the Name of the notation, another white space, either an external ID or a public ID, an optional white space, and a right-angle bracket (>), respectively. When you substitute the expression for the ExternalID rule into the notation declaration rule, you find that you have a choice between using SYSTEM with the URL of a proprietary file or PUBLIC with the public ID of a public-domain file.

Chapter 4 of *XML For Dummies* contains a primer on how to read the XML Specification. For more information in this book about the XML Specification, **see also** Part II.

You may have noticed that the structure of a notation declaration is very similar to that of an entity declaration. One thing to keep in mind with both types of declarations is that the Name and literal string denoting the ID of the file format (what follows the SYSTEM or PUBLIC) are case-sensitive.

Here are a few examples of notation declarations:

```
<!NOTATION GIF87A SYSTEM "GIF">

<!NOTATION JPEG SYSTEM "/programs/viewjpg.exe">

<!NOTATION DOC SYSTEM "winword.exe">

<!NOTATION HTML PUBLIC "-//W3C//DTD HTML 3.2//EN">
```

After you declare the name of your notation, you may use that name in entity and attribute-list declarations and in attribute specifications.

For more information about attributes and attribute declarations, *see also* Part IV. You can also find detailed information about entities and entity declarations in the section called "Entities" earlier in this part.

Part VI

Implementing XML

The best part of knowing XML is putting it into practice. This part provides practical information for using XML in your personal or professional life on a day-to-day basis. In addition to creating XML documents and document systems from the ground up, you can also convert existing documents, such as HTML or SGML documents, to XML. Once you have a set of documents, you want to manage them efficiently, serve them to your organization or to the public, and possibly publish them to other formats. If you are already familiar with the concepts and rules of XML and are anxious to put your knowledge to use, read on.

In this part . . .

- ✓ Understanding the concept of classes and groves to organize and manage a set of documents

- ✓ Converting HTML documents to XML

- ✓ Converting SGML documents to XML

- ✓ Publishing XML documents

- ✓ Serving XML

- ✓ Reading XML through a client

- ✓ Setting up server-side and client-side includes

- ✓ Maintaining an XML-based Web site or intranet

Classes and Groves

XML allows — even encourages — you to take an object-oriented approach to organizing information with its concepts of classes and groves.

A *class* is a set of objects that share similar properties. A class could be a type of logical structure, such as a set of

✦ Elements

✦ Attributes

✦ Comments

✦ Processing instructions

Each class is composed of a set of distinctive *properties* that describe the class in technical terms. For example, an element class consists of these properties:

✦ An element type Name

✦ A list of attributes

✦ Element content

In turn, each property may have its own set of distinctive properties. The content property, for instance, is composed of these properties:

✦ Character data

✦ Child elements

✦ Markup inside the element, such as

• Comments

• Processing instructions

Here's an example of an element class:

document

head

body

section

p

b

i

Each element is composed of a set of properties. The properties for document, for instance, include its child elements:

head

body

section

p

b

i

as well as its list of attributes:

author

organization

date

keyword

As you may realize, XML classes and subclasses can form a conceptual tree or set of trees. A *grove* describes the entire tree or set of trees.

Understanding the concept of classes and groves can help you design an effective system of managing XML DTDs and documents by:

✦ Eliminating unnecessary structures; in other words, "pruning" the tree.

✦ Adding important structures that you may not have thought of when first designing a DTD or document system.

✦ Making the structures, names of structures, and properties consistent.

✦ Visualizing the big picture of your document system or DTD in flow-chart style.

A complete discussion of classes and groves and managing them is beyond the scope of this book, but with this introduction, you may begin to understand how you can organize XML documents and document systems through an efficient, object-oriented approach.

For more information about character data, comments, and processing instructions, ***see also*** Part III. For more information about logical structure, elements, and attributes, ***see also*** Part IV.

You can find a list of information resources on groves in the "SGML Special Topics" section of Robin Cover's SGML/XML Web page at `www.sil.org/sgml/topics.html#groves`. In addition, you can read in-depth documentation on the schema element type, a specification that defines a class of objects, in the World Wide Web Consortium's XML-Data note at `www.w3.org/TR/1998/NOTE-XML-data/`.

Conversion

In addition to creating new XML documents from scratch, you can convert existing documents in other formats to XML. Theoretically, you can convert any document to XML — whether the original document is a 7-bit ASCII plain text file, a proprietary format such as Microsoft Word, or a public standard, like HTML or SGML.

Converting a document, formatted data, or a set of documents involves a process of massaging the textual formatting, markup, and instructions from one document format or standard to another. This process is known as *up-conversion*. Usually, up-conversion requires using software or a script that automates the conversion process, a person to make manual changes to the documents, or a combination of both.

If you have a large number of documents to convert, you may want to consider automating the process as much as possible. Setting up software or a script that automates the conversion process may be time-consuming at first, but it can save you a lot of time in the long run once you establish the system. Sometimes a person still has to look at the documents after they've gone through the automatic conversion process to make sure all the changes are correct and to see if anything needs to be added manually.

You may find that some document formats lend themselves to being converted to XML more easily than others. If, for instance, the document format that you currently use contains as much or similar markup and instructions as XML requires, your up-conversion process is easier.

One issue that can make the up-conversion process more time-consuming is that the original document format contains less information than XML requires. For instance, an original document format may contain a provision for underlined text, but the underlining itself doesn't convey the purpose of the formatting.

Using this example, underlined text could denote

✦ The title of a book

✦ An emphasized word or phrase

✦ A hyperlink

In marked-up code, these examples could appear as:

```
<title>This Boy's Life</title>

<em>An emphasized phrase that the reader should pay
    attention to</em>

<a href="http://www.w3c.org/xml/">The World Wide
    Web Consortium XML Page</a>
```

In each of these examples, the formatting of the text as it appears on-screen and in printed materials is underlined.

XML enables you to define markup for both formatting and contextual purposes; for instance, the pair of `<title>` tags conveys that the text inside the tags is a book title and that it appears as underlined text. If the format you currently use doesn't allow you to define the purpose of markup or textual formatting, you have to add this information to the original documents or to the conversion software in order to prepare the conversion process.

If you need to convert a document format that's missing a lot of structural information to an XML format that does contain a fair amount of structural information, the conversion process may require several steps:

✦ First, you can create a simple DTD based on the original document format.

✦ Next, convert the documents from their original format to XML using the DTD.

✦ Once you convert the documents to XML format, you can add markup definitions and instructions to the DTD as necessary. In other words, the DTD can evolve over time to include more structural information.

As you may expect from the definition of up-conversion, *down-conversion* is the process of converting a document or set of documents in XML to another format. Assuming that you're more interested in converting documents from a non-XML format to XML than the other way around, I don't extensively discuss down-conversion.

In addition, the sections in this part cover converting SGML and HTML documents to XML. A detailed discussion of converting documents from other formats to XML is beyond the scope of this book.

Chapters 2 and 3 of *XML For Dummies* cover the relationship of XML to HTML and SGML. For introductory information about HTML and SGML in this book, ***see also*** Part I. For more about DTDs, ***see also*** Part III. For more about markup tags, ***see also*** Part IV of this book, or Chapter 6 of *XML For Dummies.*

HTML-to-XML conversion

If you're currently authoring and serving HTML, you can learn XML fairly easily, and you can specifically learn how to convert HTML documents to XML documents.

At press time, an XML version of the HTML DTD doesn't exist yet, but Ben Trafford, a member of the HTML- and XML-development community, is developing an XML version of HTML 4.2.

According to the rules of XML, though, creating DTD-less documents is perfectly okay as long as they're well-formed. The first step in converting an HTML document to an XML document, therefore, is to make it well-formed.

One rule of well-formedness is that nonempty elements must be presented in a document with a pair of matching start- and end-tags. For example, a typical way of indicating a new paragraph in HTML is to use only a start-tag for the paragraph element p:

```
<p>New paragraph.
```

```
<p>Another new paragraph.
```

This is not acceptable. To make this well-formed, you must add matching end-tags to the paragraph (p) element:

```
<p>New paragraph.</p>
```

```
<p>Another new paragraph.</p>
```

Here are some other important steps to creating a well-formed XML document from an HTML document:

✦ Change any tags of empty elements to end with a /> closing delimiter. Typical empty elements in the header include

- ISINDEX
- BASE
- META
- LINK
- NEXTID
- RANGE

✦ Typical empty elements in the body include

- IMG
- BR
- HR
- FRAME
- WBR
- BASEFONT
- SPACER
- AUDIOSCOPE
- AREA
- PARAM
- KEYGEN
- COL
- LIMITTEXT
- SPOT
- TAB
- OVER
- RIGHT
- LEFT
- CHOOSE
- ATOP
- OF

✦ Escape markup characters with the appropriate character references; for example, the left-angle bracket (otherwise known as the less-than sign, <) appears as < and the ampersand (&) appears as &.

✦ Make sure all attribute values appear in quotes.

✦ Make sure all pairs of start- and end-tags match case and are consistent throughout the file.

✦ Make sure all attribute names are in a consistent case throughout the file.

✦ Make sure all elements nest properly and don't overlap.

In addition, correcting any syntactical errors or rough workarounds that you may have in your HTML document is important:

✦ Elements located in inappropriate places, such as a heading inside a list item or a list item outside a list environment.

✦ Inappropriate or undefined elements. This includes proprietary (browser-specific) extensions that have never been formally defined in the HTML specification.

✦ Meaningless or redundant markup that was intended to consume document space on the screen, such as

• Repeated empty paragraph elements or line breaks

• Empty tables

• Single-pixel white GIF image files

Not all changes from HTML to XML are backward compatible. For example, some HTML-based Web browsers may not accept XML-style empty elements. One workaround is to add a dummy end-tag to all empty elements.

For example, you can change this empty element for a horizontal rule (HR):

```
<HR>
```

To look like this:

```
<HR></HR>
```

It may not be the most satisfactory solution, but it's well-formed and acceptable in XML.

Once you have an HTML document that is also a well-formed XML document, you can create a basic DTD from the document. Then, gradually, you can change the HTML-specific DTD to more of an XML DTD.

For example, you can replace the HTML-specific document type declaration and any internal DTD subset with the XML declaration:

```
<?XML version="1.0" standalone="yes"?>
```

Over time, you can add new declarations for the features that you want.

For introductory information about HTML, *see also* Part I of this book, or Chapter 2 of *XML For Dummies*. For resources on HTML, *see also* the Appendix. For more information about characters, markup, and well-formedness, *see also* Part III. For more about attributes and elements, *see also* Part IV. For information about character references, *see also* Part V.

To keep up-to-date on converting HTML to XML, check Section C.5 of The XML FAQ, "How can I make my existing HTML files work in XML?" at www.ucc.ie/xml/#FAQ-EXIST.

SGML-to-XML conversion

XML is a subset of SGML, so by definition, all valid XML documents are SGML documents. Not all SGML documents are necessarily XML documents, however. SGML offers more options than XML does, and so you should be aware of some important syntactic and structural differences between SGML and XML. If you're familiar with these differences, however, converting SGML documents to XML documents isn't difficult. Assuming that you have a working familiarity with SGML, this section details the technical differences between SGML and XML, so that you can set about the task of converting SGML-compliant DTDs and documents to XML-conformant ones.

In general, here are the most significant differences between SGML and XML:

✦ XML allows documents to be simply well-formed without being valid. As long as a document is well-formed, it can be *DTD-less* — that is, a DTD, which formally defines the markup for a document, doesn't have to accompany it. This means that a document can be short and simple enough to be easily exchanged over a network, it can consume less storage space, and it can be processed more quickly. By comparison, SGML documents always require the presence of a DTD to describe the markup available to the document. SGML doesn't involve the concept of a document being well-formed without also being valid, and so it doesn't allow for DTD-less documents.

✦ XML excludes a number of markup declarations available in SGML. This simplifies the process of defining markup.

✦ XML redefines some of the internal values and parameters of SGML to make them both simpler and more flexible, such as the simplification of white-space handling.

Chapters 3, 5, and 9 of *XML For Dummies* cover SGML, DTDs, and Unicode, respectively. For introductory information about SGML in this book, ***see also*** Part I. For more about DTDs and markup declarations, ***see also*** Part III. For more about Unicode, ***see also*** Part V.

Because XML doesn't require a document to be associated with a DTD, XML provides a way to convey exact and unambiguous instructions to the XML processor regardless of whether or not a DTD accompanies a document.

One way in which XML enables a DTD-less document to be processed correctly is by differentiating the syntax of an empty element from that of a nonempty element. In XML, processors can more easily spot and parse empty elements, because empty element tags end with the predefined string /> (a slash immediately followed by a right-angle bracket). By comparison, an SGML parser must read and discern markup declarations in the DTD to differentiate empty elements from elements that contain content and include a pair of start- and end-tags.

For example, an element for a document break (BR) is an empty element. In SGML, BR would have to be defined in a DTD — and defined as an empty element so that the processor knows that the tag stands alone rather than being part of a pair. In XML, however, the processor would automatically recognize that BR is an empty element by spotting the slash (/) at the end of the element name in the tag:

```
<BR/>
```

This eliminates the need to define BR as an empty element in the DTD. As long as you use <BR/> correctly and consistently in a DTD-less document, it's well-formed and contributes to an entirely well-formed XML document. With provisions like this in XML, you may understand how the need for a DTD can be eliminated entirely.

When you're converting an SGML document to an XML document, you must find all the empty element tags and add a slash to the correct place in the tags.

For example, you must change this empty element tag for a graphic image:

```
<IMG "SRC=picture.gif">
```

to this:

```
<IMG "SRC=picture.gif"/>
```

Adding just this one character makes a big difference in terms of composing an unambiguous XML document.

For information about empty elements and tags, *see also* Part IV.

Case sensitivity is another important issue when working with XML. All the data in an XML file is case-sensitive, including both the markup and the text. By comparison, case sensitivity is optional in SGML. Case sensitivity enables you to use markup in non-Latin-alphabet programming scripts and prevents problems with *case-folding,* which is the changing of cases through an automatic process. Here are the specific rules involving case sensitivity for XML:

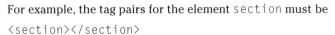

✦ Since element names used in a pair of start- and end-tags are case-sensitive, you must make sure the case in both tags match. Specifically, you must consistently use the combination of uppercase or lowercase letters defined for the element type Name, either by the DTD or by usage.

For example, the tag pairs for the element `section` must be

```
<section></section>
```

Similarly, the tag pairs for the element `SECTION` must be

```
<SECTION></SECTION>
```

Using these tag pairs is incorrect:

```
<section></SECTION>
<SECTION></section>
```

✦ In well-formed DTD-less XML files, defining the element type Name by usage means following the case of the element type Name's first instance within the document.

✦ As with start- and end-tag pairs, the case of empty element tags must also match the defined element type Name, either by the DTD or by usage.

An empty element tag for the horizontal rule element `HR`, for example, must appear as

```
<HR/>
```

and not as

```
<hr/>
<Hr/>
<hR/>
```

In fact, these tags represent four different elements:

```
<hr/>
<HR/>
<Hr/>
<hR/>
```

✦ Attribute names are case-sensitive, on a per-element basis.

For example, with the element `BACKGROUND` and the attribute `COLOR`, a conformant tag could appear as

```
<BACKGROUND COLOR="black"/>
```

According to the case definition of the attribute `COLOR`, this tag is incorrect:

```
<BACKGROUND color="black"/>
```

In fact, these tags

```
<BACKGROUND COLOR="black"/>
<BACKGROUND color="black"/>
```

represent these two different attributes, respectively:

```
COLOR
color
```

✦ The names of attribute values are also case-sensitive.

For example, this tag

```
<BACKGROUND COLOR="black"/>
```

represents a different attribute value for COLOR than this tag:

```
<BACKGROUND COLOR="BLACK"/>
```

This is important when referencing files and URLs within file systems that use case-sensitive naming conventions.

For example, these references point to three different files:

```
file.xml
File.xml
FILE.XML
```

✦ Something that SGML and XML have in common is that all entity references and data content are case-sensitive.

If you've worked with SGML extensively, you need to know which SGML constructs are excluded from XML grammar.

These SGML features are not permitted within the XML Specification:

- DATATAG
- OMITTAG
- RANK
- LINK (SIMPLE, IMPLICIT, EXPLICIT)
- CONCUR
- SUBDOC
- FORMAL

Syntactically, XML is different from SGML in these ways:

✦ XML doesn't allow short reference delimiters or these declarations:

- SHORTREF
- USEMAP

✦ The processing instruction close (PIC) delimiter in XML is ?>.

✦ XML doesn't limit quantities or capacities.

✦ Names are always case-sensitive. (In SGML, use NAMECASE NO to enable case sensitivity.)

✦ XML permits you to use underscores (_) and colons (:) in Names.

✦ XML permits you to use Unicode characters in Names, while SGML restricts you to using only ASCII characters.

Although SGML permits some exceptional constructs when the SGML feature SHORTTAG is declared as YES, you can't use these constructs in XML under any circumstances. These constructs include

✦ **Unclosed start-tags.**

For example, in this line:

```
<bold>This text appears bold.
```

the XML processor would get confused, because no end-tag indicates where the bold text should end. A start-tag must always be paired with an end-tag:

```
<bold>This text appears bold.</bold>
```

✦ **Unclosed end-tags.**

Unclosed end-tags present a similar problem to that of unclosed start-tags. This line, for example:

```
This text appears italic.</i>
```

doesn't indicate to the XML processor where the italicized text should begin. A matching pair of start- and end-tags would solve the problem:

```
<i>This text appears bold.</i>
```

✦ **Empty start-tags.** These present a similar problem as that of unclosed start-tags. The only tag that can stand alone is an empty element tag.

✦ **Empty end-tags.** End-tags cannot stand alone; again, the only tag that can stand alone is an empty element tag.

In XML, you must enter an attribute value in an attribute specification as a literal, whereas SGML allows you to enter an attribute value directly.

In XML, you can't omit the attribute Name in an attribute specification.

In addition, XML imposes a number of restrictions of features and constructs that are permitted in SGML:

+ **Attribute-list declarations:**

  - In attribute-list declarations, an associated element type can't be a name group.

  - You can't declare an attribute for a notation.

  - You can't use CURRENT attributes.

  - You can't use content reference attributes.

  - You can't use NUTOKEN(S), NUMBER(S), or NAME(S) declared values.

  - You must use the logical "or" (|) connector within a name token group.

  - In attribute-list declarations, attribute values specified as defaults must be literals.

+ **Character references:**

  - You must close a character reference with an REFC delimiter, which is the semicolon (;).

  - You may not use a named character reference in XML.

  - You may not use numeric character references to non-Unicode characters.

+ **Comments:**

  - A parameter separator can't contain comments, which means that you can't include comments within noncomment markup declarations.

  - You can't use an empty comment declaration (that is, < ! >). You must include exactly one comment in each comment declaration.

  - In a comment declaration, you can't include a white space (S) before the final MDC.

+ **Entity declarations:**

  - You can't declare a #DEFAULT entity or an external SDATA entity.

- You can't use external CDATA entities, internal SDATA entities, or internal CDATA entities.

- You can't use PI entities.

- You can't use bracketed text entities.

- You must include a system identifier in external identifiers.

- You can't specify an attribute for an entity.

- You must include the replacement text for general text entities and external parameter entities in order for the document to be well-formed.

- In a parameter literal, an ampersand must be followed by a syntactically valid entity reference or a valid numeric character reference.

✦ **Entity references:**

- You must close an entity reference with an REFC delimiter, which is the semicolon (;).

- The content of an XML document must not include any reference to external data.

- General entity references in the content of a document must be synchronous.

- Attribute values may not contain any external entity references.

- You may include a parameter entity reference in an internal DTD subset only within a declaration separator, which is a possible location for a markup declaration.

✦ **Element-type declarations:**

- In an element-type declaration, an associated element type can't be a name group.

- In an element declaration, you can't specify a generic identifier as a rank stem and rank suffix.

- You can't use minimization parameters in element declarations.

- You can't use RCDATA or CDATA declared content.

- You can't use the logical "and" (&) connector with content models.

- You must comply with the restricted form of content models for mixed content.

- You can't use inclusions or exclusions.

✦ **Marked sections:**

- In marked-section declarations, you may not use the TEMP status keyword.

- You may not use RCDATA marked sections.

- In the document instance, you may not use INCLUDE or IGNORE marked sections.

- In a marked-section declaration, a status keyword specification must contain exactly one status keyword.

- You may not use marked sections in the internal DTD subset.

- You may not use parameter separators (that is, parameter-entity references) in status keyword specifications in a document.

✦ **Processing instructions (PIs):**

- You must begin a processing instruction with a Name, which is the PI target.

- A processing instruction whose PI target is xml can only occur at the beginning of a external entity and must be an XML declaration if it's in the document entity.

- Unless it's xml, a PI target must not match [Xx][Mm][Ll] (for example, XML, xml, Xml, xMl, and so on).

✦ **Miscellaneous:**

- You may not use a Name that begins with or matches [Xx][Mm][Ll].

- In the document entity, you can't explicitly present the SGML declaration, because XML assumes it's implied.

- In data content, you must express the left-angle bracket (otherwise known as the less-than sign, ⟨) as the character reference <. Similarly, you must express the ampersand (&) as the character reference (&).

- You must include a parameter separator when it's adjacent to a delimiter.

You may use XML files directly with SGML tools, as long as

✦ The XML document is valid and accompanied by a valid DTD.

✦ The SGML software supports the XML Specification, including both the added features of XML and its restrictions.

Chapters 3 and 18 of *XML For Dummies* go into even more detail about SGML's relationship to XML. For introductory information about SGML in this book, *see also* Part I. For resources on SGML, *see also* the Appendix. For more about characters, markup, and well-formedness, *see also* Part III. For more about attributes, elements, and conditional (marked) sections, *see also* Part IV. For information about character references, entities, and notations, *see also* Part V.

For an extensive technical comparison of SGML and XML, please visit the World Wide Web Consortium's Comparison of SGML and XML by James Clark at www.w3.org/TR/NOTE-sgml-xml.

Publishing

The output of XML documents is not limited to an XML client viewed via a computer screen. As with SGML, HTML, and other document formats and specifications, you can publish XML data to a number of venues.

Output of XML data could include

- ✦ XML-compatible Web browsers
- ✦ XML-aware databases
- ✦ Printed publications, including
  - Newspapers
  - Newsletters
  - Brochures and advertising materials
  - Magazines
  - Books
  - Reference materials
  - Custom and personal publications
- ✦ Computer help files
- ✦ Software products, including
  - Multimedia products
  - Programming scripts that interpret XML data
- ✦ CD-ROMs
- ✦ Newsfeeds

You can probably think of other ways to use XML in addition to the ideas on this list. Theoretically, you can use XML in any form of data transfer or document exchange, which is a great reason to learn and use it.

Serving XML

One of the main purposes of using XML is to create documents and data that conform to a technical standard, so that you can share your documents with others and you can read their documents in the same format. Thus, when you work with XML, you probably want to set up a system that stores, manages, and shares XML DTDs and documents for more than one person. A system that works best is usually a client-server system, usually modeled after typical file-sharing servers and Internet servers. An ideal solution is a client-server system running over a TCP/IP-based network (that is, a network that uses standard Internet protocols) that includes both server and client XML-aware software.

Clients (and client-side includes)

Because XML is a specification that you can use on any platform and over a network, most developers of XML products focus on creating platform-independent, fully networkable XML-savvy systems. At this point, therefore, most XML clients are emerging in the form of Web browsers or Java applications, including Web browser plug-ins and products for Java-enabled Web browsers.

If you manage a Web site or an intranet that includes XML documents, or you develop the technical aspects of the content for your organization, you may be interested in using client-side includes. A *client-side include* is an instruction or set of instructions embedded within a document that processes some type of data on or within the client.

You can use client-side includes in XML as long as any embedded code passed to a third-party engine or interface doesn't contain any characters that can be misinterpreted as XML markup. Third-party engines and interfaces include

- ✦ Structured Document Query Language (SDQL) inquiries
- ✦ Java input
- ✦ Netscape LiveWire requests
- ✦ Streamed data content

To prevent characters from being misinterpreted as XML markup, you have two options:

+ Use CDATA sections to hold XML-specific code. CDATA sections provide a "safe zone" for XML code by telling the XML application to avoid parsing it.

+ Use character and entity references instead of markup characters. For instance, substitute < for the left-angle bracket (<).

As long as you take these precautions, you can configure a powerful system that integrates XML with other types of data and data-processing engines.

For more information about CDATA sections, *see also* Part III. For more about character and entity references, *see also* Part V.

A list of currently available and new XML-aware products, including clients, is posted to the XML Industry Support section of the SGML/XML Web page at www.sil.org/sgml/xmlSupport.html.

Servers (and server-side includes)

Once you have a number of XML files, you need a way to share them with others. An efficient way to share XML files is to store, organize, and serve them from a server on a network. In fact, an organization of people who need to effectively share XML files with each other must have access to one or a number of XML-enabled servers.

If you want to set up a system to host and serve XML documents, you may not have to purchase additional equipment and software if you already have an Internet or intranet server in place. You can serve XML files fairly easily by making a few changes to the server software settings.

To serve XML documents, which are usually identified as files with an .xml or .XML extension, you must add the correct Multipurpose Internet Mail Extensions (MIME) type to the MIME-types configuration file or list.

For your server to recognize an XML MIME type, add this line to the MIME-types configuration file or list:

```
text/xml    xml XML
```

If you use Extensible Style Language (XSL), you can configure your server to recognize XSL files by adding this line to the MIME-types configuration file or list:

```
text/xsl    xsl XSL
```

Your XML documents may reference one or several types of adjunct files, such as

✦ A DTD

✦ An entity file containing either

• Parseable XML data

• Binary data

✦ A catalog

✦ A style sheet

Each of these adjunct file types may require its own MIME entry in the MIME-types configuration file. Also, you must place each adjunct file in the appropriate directory referenced by the XML document.

For more information about DTDs, *see also* Part III. For more about entities, *see also* Part V. For more about XSL, check out Chapter 8 of *XML For Dummies,* and *see also* the Appendix of this book. For more on editing the MIME-types configuration file on your server, consult the manual for your server.

If you currently manage an entirely HTML-based document system you may be using one or a number of scripts to automatically generate HTML documents. You don't necessarily need to rewrite all of your scripts to accommodate XML. If you're transitioning from an HTML-based document system to an XML-based system or to an XML/HTML hybrid system, you must modify the scripts to produce the relevant document type for XML. You can accomplish this by simply changing the document type declaration from HTML to the appropriate XML type.

For example, this is a common HTML document type declaration:

```
<!DOCTYPE HTML PUBLIC "-//W3C//DTD HTML 3.2 Final/
    EN">
```

Simply change this to an XML-specific document type declaration:

```
<!DOCTYPE rootElementName PUBLIC "URL">
```

Chapter 2 of *XML For Dummies* explains HTML's relationship to XML. For more information about HTML in this book, *see also* Part I. You also can find more on converting HTML to XML in the "HTML-to-XML conversion" subsection of the "Conversion" section earlier in this part. For more about document type declarations, *see also* Part III.

A *server-side include (SSI)* automatically and immediately parses and generates documents and sends them to client applications. If you have any SSIs running on your server, you may continue to use them with XML as long as the SSI scripts generate XML-conformant files that are either valid or well-formed.

For more information about validity and well-formedness, ***see also*** Part III of this book, or Chapter 5 of *XML For Dummies.*

An in-depth discussion of server-side includes is beyond the scope of this book, but you can find detailed information on SSIs in the NCSA HTTPd Server Side Includes (SSI) Tutorial at `hoohoo.ncsa.uiuc.edu/docs/tutorials/includes.html` or in Mark West's SSI Tutorial at `www.carleton.ca/~dmcfet/html/ssi3.html`. In addition, the official Web site for the popular HTTP server project Apache is at `www.apache.org`.

Site Maintenance

If you manage a Web site or intranet for your organization, you may consider transitioning from an entirely HTML-based Web site to a hybrid XML/HTML Web site. You can manage a Web site or intranet manually, but if the site grows, you probably want to use a software product to maintain all of your DTDs, documents, and data.

This type of product is often called a document management system. A *document management system* enables you to manage and serve a large number of documents as well as data that is classified in multiple ways.

Here are some important features and functions to look for in a document management system:

✦ You may configure a central repository or a directory in which you store documents.

✦ You may set access rights for users.

✦ It allows for library-style document checkout, and it locks documents when they're being accessed and edited to prevent the creation of multiple versions of the same document.

✦ It logs edits to documents and data.

✦ It automates publishing and report-generation from a set of documents or data.

✦ It accounts for both the physical structure and the logical structure of your documents and allows you to organize the entities and elements of a set of documents.

A number of software manufacturers are currently working on document management systems for XML. Some document management systems may support SGML, HTML, and other document types.

 A list of currently available and new XML-aware products is posted to the XML Industry Support section of the SGML/XML Web page at `www.sil.org/sgml/xmlSupport.html`.

XML Resources and Future Developments

Because XML is a relatively new specification, it may undergo many changes pertaining to both itself and to its related technologies. This appendix provides a number of resources in which you can seek additional information and stay abreast of developments in the world of XML. The resources listed in this appendix include books, tools, and Web sites.

Also, many XML-compatible technologies and specifications were developed concurrently or soon after the initial development of XML. Because the XML Specification itself was finalized only recently, the number of XML-related technologies available now is a testament to the promise and potential of XML. Sections of this appendix explore the multidirectional developments of XML and XML-related technologies.

Bibliography

Sometimes, the best way to find out something new is the old-fashioned way — read a book and study the subject matter in depth. The following list includes current and soon-to-be released books on XML or XML-related subjects:

+ ***Designing XML Internet Applications:*** Michael Leventhal, David Lewis, and Matthew Fuchs; Prentice Hall; 0136168221.

+ ***Hand on XML:*** Rob Tidrow; Prima Publishing; 0761515356.

+ ***Implementing CDF Channels:*** McGraw-Hill; 0070498873. A guide to using Microsoft's Channel Definition Format (CDF).

+ ***Instant XML Programmer's Reference:*** Trevor Jenkins; Wrox Press, Inc.; 1861001525. A reference guide to XML for programmers.

+ ***Practical Guide to SGML/XML Filters:*** Norman E. Smith; Wordware Publishing; 1556225873.

+ ***Presenting XML:*** Richard Light; SAMS.NET (Sams Publishing/ Macmillan Publishing); 1575213346. An introduction and reference to XML. Web site: `www.mcp.com/info/1-57521/ 1-57521-334-6/`.

+ ***SGML Buyer's Guide: A Unique Guide to Determining Your Requirements and Choosing the Right SGML and XML Products and Services:*** Charles F. Goldfarb, Steve Pepper, and Chet Ensign; Prentice Hall; 0136815111. An extensive, 1,000+-page guide with CD-ROM and a "Sponsor Showcase."

+ ***The SGML FAQ Book: Understanding the Foundation of HTML and XML:*** Steven J. Derose; Kluwer Academic Publishing; 0792399439.

+ ***Structuring XML Documents:*** David Megginson; Prentice Hall; 0136422993.

+ ***Teach Yourself XML in 21 Days:*** James K. Tauber; SAMS.NET (Sams Publishing/Macmillan Publishing); 1575213966. An extensive tutorial covering XML, CDF, electronic commerce, and the Mathematical Markup Language (MathML).

+ ***Using XML:*** Patricia Ju; Que; 0789714086. A technical reference and tutorial.

+ ***Web Publishing with XML in Six Easy Steps:*** Bryan Pfaffenberger; AP Professional; 0125531664.

+ ***XML: A Primer:*** Simon St. Laurent; MIS Press/IDG Books; 155828592X. An introduction and guide to XML, including XML-related languages and standards.

✦ *XML: Extensible Markup Language:* Justin Higgins and Ruth Maran; IDG Books Worldwide; 0764531999. A guide to developing Web pages and browser-independent extensions with XML; includes a CD-ROM.

✦ *XML by Example: A Webmaster's Guide:* Sean McGrath; Prentice Hall; 0139601627.

✦ *XML Complete:* Steven Holzner; McGraw-Hill; 0079137024. A how-to development guide with CD-ROM.

✦ *XML For Dummies:* Ed Tittel, Norbert Mikula, and Ramesh Chandak; IDG Books Worldwide, Inc; 076450360X. An overview and reference to XML; the larger companion to this Quick Reference.

✦ *XML Handbook:* Charles F. Goldfarb and Paul Prescod; Prentice Hall; 0130811521.

✦ *XML: Principles, Tools, and Techniques:* Dan Connolly; O'Reilly & Associates, Inc.; 1565923499. A collection of articles about XML from the *World Wide Web Journal*.

Tools

The following is a list of XML development tools and XML-aware products available on the market or in the public domain.

Tool name: vendor/author; supported platforms; URL.

✦ **ADEPT Editor:** Arbor Text, Inc.; UNIX, Windows NT/95, OS2; www.arbortext.com/editor.html.

✦ **Ælfred:** Microstar; Java; www.microstar.com/XML/.

✦ **Astoria:** Chrystal Software; N/A; Sun Solaris and Windows NT/95; www.chrystal.com/product.htm.

✦ **Balise:** AIS Software; UNIX, Windows 3.*x*/NT/95; www.balise.berger-levrault.fr/current/.

✦ **DAE SDK:** Copernican Solutions, Inc.; Java; www.copsol.com/products/dae/.

✦ **DataChannel XML Development Environment (DXDE):** DataChannel; any with a Java runtime available; free; www.datachannel.com/products/xml/.

✦ **DXP - DataChannel XML Parser:** Norbert H. Mikula, DataChannel; any with a Java runtime available; www.datachannel.com/products/xml/DXP/.

✦ **DynaBase; DynaText:** Inso; N/A; www.inso.com/.

- **FrameMaker:** Adobe; Windows 95 and NT, Macintosh, UNIX; `www.adobe.com/aboutadobe/publicrelations/HTML/9712/971209.xml.html`

- **HoTMetaL Application Server:** SoftQuad; Solaris, SGI-IRIX, Linux, UNIX, FreeBSD, Windows 95/NT; `www.softquad.com/products/hotmetal/hmapps.htm`.

- **Insight:** Enigma; Windows 95 and NT; `www.enigmainc.com/xmlpr.htm`.

- **Interaction Web Server Companion:** Interaction in Progress; Macintosh; `interaction.in-progress.com/`.

- **Jumbo:** Peter Murray-Rust; Java-enabled Web browser; `www.venus.co.uk/~pmr/README`.

- **Konstructor:** OmniMark; N/A; `www.omnimark.com/xml-start.html`.

- **Lark:** Tim Bray; Java runtime; `www.textuality.com/Lark/`

- **LT XML:** Language Technology Group; UNIX, Windows NT/95, Macintosh; `www.ltg.ed.ac.uk/software/xml/`.

- **Microsoft XML Parser in Java:** Microsoft, Inc.; any with Java Virtual Machine Installed; `www.microsoft.com/workshop/author/xml/parser/`.

- **Symposia doc+:** Grif S.A; UNIX, AIX, Windows NT/95; `www.grif.fr/`.

- **TclXML:** Advanced Computational Systems; any with Tcl version 8.0b1 or later; `tcltk.anu.edu.au/XML/`.

- **Web Automation Toolkit:** webMethods; UNIX, Windows NT/95, Macintosh; `www.webmethods.com/`.

- **WebWriter:** STILO; Windows; `www.stilo.com/products/xmlbody.htm`.

- **XML:: Parser Perl Module:** Larry Wall; Perl environments; `ftp:www.wall.org/pub/larry/xmlparser-o.o.tar.gz`

- **XML Repository:** POET Software; N/A; `www.poet.com/xml.html`

- **XML Styler:** ArborText; Windows95/NT with Internet Explorer 4.0; `www.arbortext.com/xmlstyler/`.

Web Sites

If you're looking for up-to-the-minute information on XML and XML-related technology, you want to frequent the Web. You can find just about any information regarding XML on the Web, including general information, lists of Frequently Asked Questions

(FAQs), introductions and tutorials, and lists of information resources, including superlists of Web sites and online bibliographies.

XML-Related Web Resources

Name	URL
A Technical Introduction to XML	`www.arbortext.com/nwalsh.html`
ArborText XML Resources	`www.arbortext.com/xmlresrc.html`
Cascading Style Sheets	`www.w3.org/TR/REC-CSS1`
Channel Definition Format (CDF) — Microsoft	`www.microsoft.com/standards/cdf.htm`
Channel Definition Format (CDF) — W3C	`www.w3.org/TR/NOTE-CDFsubmit.html`
Charles F. Goldfarb's SGML Source Home Page	`www.sgmlsource.com/`
Chemical Markup Language (CML)	`www.venus.co.uk/omf/cml/doc/`
DataChannel's XML Page	`datachannel.com/channelworld/XML/XMLIndex.htm`
Document Object Model (DOM)	`www.w3.org/DOM/`
Document Style Semantics and Specification Language (DSSSL)	`www.jclark.com/dsssl/`
Extensible Linking Language (XLL/XLink)	`www.sil.org/sgml/xll.html`
Extensible Markup Language (XML) 1.0 W3C Recommendation	`www.w3.org/TR/REC-xml`
Extensible Markup Language Frequently Asked Questions, or XML FAQ	`www.textuality.com/xml/faq.html`
Extensible Style Language (XSL)	`www.w3.org/Style/XSL/`
Frequently Asked Questions about the Extensible Markup: The XML FAQ	`www.ucc.ie/xml/`
Graphic Communications Association	`www.gca.org/`
HyTime Users' Group Home Page	`www.hytime.org/`
International Organization for Standardization (ISO)	`www.iso.ch/`
Mathematical Markup Language: W3C Working Draft	`www.w3.org/TR/WD-math/`
Microsoft's XML Pages	`www.microsoft.com/standards/xml/`

(continued)

Name	*URL*
OpenTag	`www.opentag.org/otdownld.htm`
Presenting XML, Appendix B: Bibliography	`www.mcp.com/files/1-57521/1-57521-334-6/resource.htm`
Resource Description Framework (RDF)	`www.w3.org/RDF/Overview.html`
SGML Bibliography	`www.sil.org/sgml/bib-strt.html`
SGML FAQ	`www.infosys.utas.edu.au/info/sgmlfaq.txt`
SGML Resource Center's XML Information	`www.mcs.net/~dken/xml.htm`
SGML/XML Web Page, The	`www.sil.org/sgml/xml.html`
Synchronized Multimedia Integration Language (SMIL)	`www.whatis.com/smil.htm`
Textuality's XML Site	`www.textuality.com/xml/`
Unicode Consortium	`www.unicode.org/`
VSMS JAVA-XML Home Page	`ala.vsms.nottingham.ac.uk/vsms/java/`
W3C Technical Reports & Publications	`www.w3.org/TR/`
W3C XML Linking Language (XLink)	`www.w3.org/TR/WD-xlink`
Web Review, "A Guide to XML Resources"	`webreview.com/97/05/16/feature/xmlguide.html`
Web Style Sheets	`www.w3.org/Style/`
What Is XLL?	`www.stg.brown.edu/~sjd/xllintro.html`
What Is XML?	`www.gca.org/conf/xml/xml_what.htm`
What the <?XML!>	`www.geocities.com/SiliconValley/Peaks/5957/xml.html`
What's the Point of XML?	`www.sun.com/sunworldonline/swol-02-1998/swol-02-xml.html`
World Wide Web Consortium (W3C) XML Page	`www.w3.org/xml/`

Name	URL
XML Developer's Mailing List Archive	`www.lists.ic.ac.uk/ hypermail/xml-dev/`
XML Industry Support	`www.sil.org/sgml/ xmlSupport.html`
XML News	`www.sil.org/sgml/ xmlNews.html`
XML Resources from ArborText	`www.arbortext.com/ xmlresrc.html`
XML, Java, and the Future of the Web	`www.sunsite.unc.edu/ pub/sun-info/ standards/xml/why/ xmlapps.htm`
XML/EDI (Electronic Data Interchange)	`www.geocities.com/ WallStreet/Floor/5815/`
XML: The Extensible Markup Language, James K. Tauber	`www.jtauber.com/xml/`
XML: The New Markup Wave	`www.csclub.uwaterloo. ca/u/relander/XML/ Wave/`
Yahoo!'s XML Category	`www.yahoo.com/ Computers_and_ Internet/ Information_and_ Documentation/Data_ Formats/XML/`

XML Developments on the Horizon

No technology works in a vacuum, and XML especially lends itself well to working with other specifications and tools, including style sheet specifications, standard markup languages, and conventional programming languages. XML, in conjunction with other technologies, has a synergistic effect; with some savvy, you can experience the best of both worlds — with XML and with the related technology you use. Check out this section to discover the multidirectional developments of XML and XML-related technologies.

To keep up with XML applications and industry initiatives on your own, check out `www.sil.org/sgml/xml.html#applications`.

Channel Definition Format (CDF)

The Channel Definition Format (CDF) is the first commercial application of XML. Microsoft developed CDF to name and specify Web-based collections of information that are frequently or continually updated — or *channels*. A Web server automatically delivers the information to computers with compatible receiver programs. Microsoft first implemented CDF in Internet Explorer 4.0.

The World Wide Web Consortium (W3C) defines the following terms in reference to the design and intent of CDF:

Terms for the Original Design and Intent of the CDF

Term	Definition
Automatic	The user chooses a channel once; thereafter, scheduled deliveries of information to the client occurs without further user intervention.
Standard Web server	Any Web server that uses the HTTP 1.0 or later protocol can broadcast channels.
Compatible	Any program that processes and retrieves content according to the W3C specification of CDF.

CDF serves as a local index to a channel's available content when the content downloads to a client. One use of the CDF could involve an implicit hierarchy in a CDF — like a multi-tiered table of contents — within a channel selector that is accurately presented to the user by a client application.

The CDF contains several major elements that are explicitly defined by the W3C specification. You may define each CDF element (and attribute) using an XML declaration. The following lists the major elements of the CDF:

The CDF Major Elements

Element	The Object It Defines
Channel	A channel
Item	A channel item, which is a unit of information available from a channel
UserSchedule	A reference to a specified schedule of a client or user
Schedule	A specified schedule
Logo	An image representing a channel or channel item
Tracking	User-tracking parameters of a channel
CategoryDef	A category, which could be a child category of another category

For each of these major elements, you may apply a number of relevant minor elements. With a CDF-compliant DTD, you can easily create a document or entire class of documents by implementing the principles of XML; then you can put each document into practice as a fully functional channel.

For more information about CDF, visit the Microsoft CDF Web page at `www.microsoft.com/standards/cdf.htm`. For more information about the CDF as defined by the World Wide Web Consortium, including a sample channel document, visit the W3C CDF page at `www.w3.org/TR/NOTE-CDFsubmit.html`.

Java and XML

Java is a robust object-oriented programming language developed by Sun Microsystems. One of the best features of Java is that it allows you to write a program on one platform and automatically run it on any other platform, which makes it ideal for running programs over the Internet.

Because both Java and XML transfer information over any computer system, the combination of Java and XML form a powerful development environment for platform-independent and even software-independent applications. Many tools for XML development, such as editors and XML clients, are in fact Java-based — allowing you to compose and view XML documents in any Java runtime environment.

Combining Java with XML is relatively new, so it's fair to say that most of the Java-XML applications haven't been developed yet, and probably haven't even been conceived of yet. Just a few of the possibilities of using Java in conjunction with XML include

- ✦ Multimedia data

- ✦ Shared trade notebooks

- ✦ Public and private data channels

- ✦ Multiuser calendars and personal information managers

- ✦ Java-aware markup languages

- ✦ Networked database applications

A recently developed markup language that involves both Java and XML is the Java Speech Markup Language (JSML) Specification. JSML is designed to enable "applications to annotate text with additional information that can improve the quality and natural-ness of synthesized speech." With JSML, you can

- ✦ Include structural information about paragraphs and sentences within documents.

- ✦ Control the production of synthesized speech, including

  - • The pronunciation of words and phrases.

  - • The emphasis of words, such as stressing or accenting.

- The placements of boundaries and pauses.

- The control of pitch and speaking rate.

✦ Embed markers in text and enable synthesizer-specific controls.

JSML represents an exciting new potential for XML — one that exceeds the use of simple textual data and enters the realm of speech, a basic but complex human interface. Since JSML is an application of XML, developing isn't hard once you understand the concepts of XML.

For more information about Java, visit `java.sun.com/`. For more information about Java and XML, read "XML, Java, and the Future of the Web" at `sunsite.unc.edu/pub/sun-info/standards/ xml/why/xmlapps.html`. For more information about JSML, visit `java.sun.com/products/java-media/speech/ forDevelopers/JSML/`.

Markup languages

Knowing XML isn't very useful unless you intend to create something with it. The result of what you create with XML is an application, usually in the form of a specific markup language. Markup languages are the bread and butter of document management and exchange.

Currently, a number of XML-derived markup languages are available and in development. This section briefly discusses two of the most notable and earliest-developed markup languages designed for use in particular industries: Chemical Markup Language (CML) and Mathematical Markup Language (MathML).

Chemical Markup Language. Created by Peter Murray-Rust, Chemical Markup Language (CML) was the first application of XML to be developed.

CML is a precise XML dialect that enables chemists to manipulate and model atoms and molecules as data elements. Catering to the needs of researchers and academics, CML supports a number of standard document elements for scholarly papers, such as

✦ Footnotes

✦ Citations

✦ Mathematical and chemical formulas

✦ Glossary terms

As the earliest application of XML, CML aptly and undeniably demonstrates the power of XML. Although the specification for

CML is under a dozen pages long, it enables you to clearly document any type of chemical data or formula.

To use and view CML documents, you can use the Java-based browser, Jumbo, also written by Peter Murray-Rust.

For more information about CML, visit www.venus.co.uk/omf/cml/doc/. For more information about Jumbo, read the README file at www.venus.co.uk/~pmr/README.

Chapter 10 of *XML For Dummies* covers Chemical Markup Language in detail, if you want to find out more about this XML-based language.

Mathematical Markup Language (MathML). Mathematical Markup Language (MathML) is an XML-derived markup language used to describe mathematical notation, capture both its structure and content, and exchange mathematical data over the Web. MathML presents a savvy solution to expressing complex mathematical notation and expressions over a network and in multiple computer environments.

The design goals of MathML include the following capabilities:

✦ Encoding mathematical material suitable for teaching and scientific communication at all levels.

✦ Encoding both mathematical notation and mathematical meaning.

✦ Facilitating conversion to and from other math formats, both presentational and semantic, although conversion to and from other notational systems or media may lose information in the process. Output formats include

- Graphical displays

- Speech synthesizers

- Computer algebra systems input

- Math layout languages, such as TeX

- Plain-text displays, such as VT100 emulators

- Print media, including Braille

✦ Transferring information to specific renderers and applications.

✦ Efficient browsing for lengthy expressions.

✦ Extensibility.

✦ Using templates and other math-editing techniques.

✦ Simplifying software generation and processing and ease in human legibility.

Note that the robustness and design of MathML lend themselves well to use with equation editors, conversion programs, and other specialized software tools to generate MathML data, rather than direct use by authors. In this way, MathML is an excellent example of an XML application created to be an obscured layer of information system management sandwiched between the information and the user.

For more information about MathML, visit the MathML W3C Working Draft at `www.w3.org/TR/WD-math/`.

Chapter 14 of *XML For Dummies* covers MathML in detail, if you're interested in finding out more about this XML-based language.

OpenTag

Designed by the International Language Engineering Corporation (ILE), OpenTag enables you to deliver the content of XML documents to readers of different languages.

OpenTag is based on a system of encoding text, which is extracted from documents of different formats, and automatically reusing the previously translated text.

The steps for using OpenTag for translation include

✦ Abstracting the heterogeneous formatting information of a file into OpenTag markup

✦ Composing homogeneously tagged text files, regardless of the original file format

✦ Extracting the data from the original format

✦ Manipulating the data in an OpenTag environment

✦ Merging the data back into the original format

This process, referred to as *Translation Memory,* essentially enables you to translate the first version of a document and store each original sentence of the document in a database along with its translation. After the first translation, the translation memory engine queries the database with sentences from new document versions to find matches from the original text. When it finds a match, it retrieves the corresponding translation for use with the new translated text. In this way, OpenTag automates the process of language translation.

As you may agree, OpenTag is an ingenious use of XML for tightening the gap between multiple languages over computer networks.

For more information about OpenTag, visit `www.opentag.org/`.

Perl and XML

Perl, an acronym for Practical Extraction and Report Language, is a programming language widely used in Internet and private network applications on UNIX, Windows, and Macintosh platforms. Larry Wall developed Perl, a freely available code, to excel at text processing.

Members of the Perl and the XML development communities believe that Perl and XML can work together very well and form a powerful combination for text-manipulation and data-management applications. For this reason, Perl developers are making XML "the language of choice for those doing 'structured' text processing."

The potential uses for integrating Perl with XML include

+ Using Perl to create efficient scripts and programs for processing XML documents and data

+ Storing documents in open, nonproprietary formats

+ Using Perl with different human languages

+ Scripting Perl to automatically retrieve and manipulate data from XML-compatible databases

At press time, a number of technical issues need to be resolved before Perl can be fully utilized with XML, such as integrating the Unicode standard into Perl so that it can accept XML-compliant character encoding schemes.

For more information about Perl, visit www.perl.com/. For more information about Perl and XML, read "Perl Support for XML Developing: How to Make Perl the Language of Choice for XML" at www.perl.com/perl-xml.html.

Resource Description Framework (RDF) and Metadata

Resource Description Framework (RDF) is a W3C initiative for uniting and standardizing three different applications:

+ The PICS dialect, which is the W3C standard for defining graphics data

+ Netscape Meta Content Framework (MCF), which defines a general-purpose metadata language

+ Microsoft XML-Data, which also defines a general-purpose metadata language but which is incompatible with MCF or PICS

Its design goals include these features:

+ Interoperability of metadata

+ Machine-understandable semantics for metadata

+ A uniform query capability for resource discovery

+ Better precision in resource discovery than full text search

+ A processing-rules language for automated decision-making about Web resources

+ A language for retrieving metadata from third parties

+ Future-proofing applications, as schemas evolve

Some potential applications of RDF metadata include

+ Using resource discovery to provide better search-engine capabilities

+ Cataloging and describing the content and content relationships available at a Web site

+ Sharing and exchanging information using intelligent software agents

+ Describing collections of pages that represent a single logical document for use in content rating

+ Describing intellectual property rights of Web pages

+ Using digital signatures for electronic commerce and organizations

At press time, RDF is still in development, which includes the integration of XML.

For more information about RDF, visit the W3C RDF page at www.w3.org/RDF/. For more information about metadata, visit the W3C Metadata and Resource Description page at www.w3.org/Metadata/.

Chapter 12 of *XML For Dummies* has a great deal of information about RDF. Check it out!

Style and style sheets

A *style sheet* is a technical description for the presentation of documents on computer screens, in print, or even in speech pronunciation. Styles and style sheets aren't new concepts in designing and managing textual data, but efforts to standardize style sheets for use on the Internet is a relatively recent development. Soon, Web browsers will be able to accept style sheets, and users will be able to view documents in any predesigned style.

By attaching a style sheet to an XML-structured document, authors and readers can influence how the document is presented without sacrificing device-independence or having to add new markup tags.

This section discusses three efforts to standardize style sheets: Cascading Style Sheet Specification (CSS), Document Style and Semantics Specification Language (DSSSL), and Extensible Style Language (XSL).

For more information about standard styles and style sheets, visit the W3C Web Style Sheets page at www.w3.org/Style/.

Cascading Style Sheets (CSS) is a simple mechanism for adding style to Web documents — specifically HTML.

Styles could involve

- ✦ Fonts
- ✦ Colors
- ✦ Headings
- ✦ Spacing
- ✦ Box properties
- ✦ Classification properties
- ✦ Vertical and horizontal formatting

CSS is easy to learn and quite intuitive, especially if you're used to formatting and desktop publishing design. One of the most important features of CSS is that style sheets *cascade* — that is, an author can attach a preferred style sheet, while the reader may use a personal style sheet that adjusts for human or technological handicaps.

CSS works very well with HTML, but you can also use it with XML, as long as your XML document has a linear structure that can be displayed without extensive manipulation.

Right now, CSS is somewhat of a competing standard with Extensible Style Language (XSL), which was designed especially for use with XML. If you are familiar with CSS, however, you're at an advantage to learning other style sheet standards, such as XSL.

For more information about CSS, visit the W3C CCS page at www.w3.org/Style/css/ and the Cascading Style Sheets, Level 1 page at www.w3.org/TR/REC-CSS1.

If you're interested in finding out more about CSS, check out Chapter 8 of *XML For Dummies*.

Document Style and Semantics Specification Language (DSSSL) is an international standard for associating processing, which involves formatting and transformation, with SGML documents.

DSSSL consists of a number of components:

+ **The style language,** which describes the formatting of SGML documents.

+ **Flow objects,** which describe the layout of a document, including such constructs as

  • Page sequences

  • Paragraphs

  • Hyperlinks

  • Artwork

  Flow objects also describe the characteristics for each of these constructs:

  • A page sequence's margins

  • A paragraph's font size

  • A hyperlink's destination

  • A picture's height and width

+ **The Transformation Language,** which is a standard language for transforming an SGML document containing the markup of one DTD into a document marked up according to another DTD.

+ **A document model,** corresponding with the HyTime standard, which describes a document or a set of documents as *nodes* organized into a *grove.*

+ **The Query Language,** which selects and returns document components — specifically, nodes from the DSSSL/HyTime document model.

To put DSSSL into practice, you can use Jade, James Clark's implementation of the DSSSL style language.

DSSSL formed the basis of the development of Extensible Style Language (XSL).

For more information about DSSSL, visit James Clark's DSSSL page at www.jclark.com/dsssl/. For more information about Jade, visit www.jclark.com/jade/. For more information about HyTime, visit the HyTime Users' Group Home Page at www.hytime.org/.

If you want to know more aobut DSSSL, check out Chapter 8 of *XML For Dummies.*

Extensible Style Language (XSL), which was developed from the collective knowledge of and experience with CSS and DSSSL, is a new user-extensible and declarative standard for use with XML documents. XSL offers an excellent adjunct to XML, especially for highly structured and data-rich documents that require extensive formatting.

As with CSS, styles defined by XSL could involve

✦ Fonts

✦ Colors

✦ Headings

✦ Spacing

✦ Box properties

✦ Classification properties

✦ Vertical and horizontal formatting

At press time, XSL is still in the experimental phase of development.

For more information about XSL, visit the W3C XSL page at `www.w3.org/Style/XSL/`.

For more detailed information on XSL, check out Chapter 8 of *XML For Dummies.*

Synchronized Multimedia Interface Definition Language (SMIL)

Synchronized Multimedia Interface Definition Language (SMIL, pronounced "smile") enables Web site developers to easily define and synchronize multimedia elements for Web presentation and interaction. Using SMIL, you can send multimedia elements separately but coordinate their timing.

Multimedia elements could include

✦ Video

✦ Audio

✦ Fixed graphic images

Some of the impressive features of SMIL include these capabilities:

✦ Storing a media object in multiple versions, each with a different bandwidth assignment

✦ Delivering multiple language versions of soundtracks

✦ Entering simple description statements into a low-tech application such as a plain-text editor

In addition, SMIL makes using XML in multimedia presentations easy: You can describe a presentation using only three XML elements for multimedia types. SMIL represents a promising alternative to proprietary multimedia management systems.

For more information about SMIL, visit `www.whatis.com/ smil.htm` and the W3C Audio, Video, and Synchronized Multimedia page at `www.w3.org/AudioVideo/`.

If you want more details on SMIL and how to use it, see Chapter 16 of *XML For Dummies*.

XML Linking Language (XLL or XLink)

XML Linking Language (also called XLL or, more commonly XLink) — sometimes referred to as Extensible Linking Specification, XLink, or XML Part 2 — defines a flexible and robust set of syntax and semantics for hyperlinking within XML documents. Specifically, XLink increases the IQ of hyperlinking by implementing more sophisticated multi-ended, typed, and self-describing links than the simple unidirectional hyperlinks of HTML.

The impressive features of XLink include these capabilities:

✦ Traversing various kinds of named links

✦ Instructing a single link to coordinate multiple updates to different regions of the display screen

✦ Invoking a variety of special processing when particular links are selected

Since hyperlinking is a vital part of Web and intranet documents, XLink is a crucial component to implementing XML. In fact, XLink is sometimes called XML Part 2 because it represents the natural complement to XML itself.

At press time, the XLink Specification is still in the working-draft phase of the W3C.

For more information about XLink, visit `www.sil.org/sgml/ xll.html`. To view the W3C XLink Specification, visit `www.w3.org/TR/WD-xml-link`.

XLink is still being considered by the W3C, but you can find out more about it in Chapter 7 of *XML For Dummies*.

Techie Talk

application: The software that enables you to use and view XML documents. Applications generally involve an XML processor or parser, which enables you to manipulate and generate documents. Another definition for the term *application* is a markup language derived from XML; for example, Chemical Markup Language (CML) and Mathematical Markup Language (MathML) are both XML applications.

attribute: A piece of descriptive data that defines and constrains an element. Technically, an attribute consists of a name-value pair that is applied to an element. Also referred to as an **attribute specification.**

attribute default: The value of an attribute inherited from the DTD when a new value is not explicitly specified for that attribute within a document.

attribute list: A set of more than one attribute. Within a set, each attribute specification has its own name-value pair. In addition, a space separates each attribute.

attribute-list declaration: A declaration that defines and constrains one or more attributes, or characteristics of an element.

attribute specification: *See* **attribute.**

attribute type: The function of an attribute. To produce a valid document, all the values for each attribute must be the correct type; that is, they must match what's declared for them.

base character: An alphabetic character of the Latin alphabet, without diacritics.

binary: *See* **unparsed.**

binary entity: *See* **unparsed entity.**

boundary of an element: The outer edges of an element; in the case of a nonempty element, the boundary is marked by the start- and end-tags delimiting the element within the document.

browser: A client application used to view HTML and/or XML documents on the Web or an intranet.

Byte Order Mark (BOM): The appropriate encoding signature that begins an entity within the UTF-16 character encoding scheme. The BOM is a special character indicated by the hexadecimal value FEFF (denoted as #xFEFF), which tells the XML processor to byte-swap character code elements. The byte-reversed value of this character's code — in other words, its associated character if it had one — is a special code value that isn't assigned to a character. The XML processor uses the BOM to differentiate between UTF-8 and UTF-16 encoded documents, and it doesn't consider this encoding signature part of either the markup or the character data of the XML document.

case: The typographic class of letters in the alphabet. In the Latin alphabet, case is divided into two classes: uppercase (capital) letters and lowercase letters.

case sensitivity: The ability of a software program to discriminate between uppercase and lowercase letters.

CDATA section: A marked section of a DTD that includes literal data that the XML processor ignores.

character: The smallest and most basic unit of textual data. In XML, a character is a single data chunk of physical structure.

character class: The set of characters that forms the basis of XML data. XML conforms to the Unicode standard and groups characters into several distinctive classes: base characters, ideographic characters, combining characters, digits, and extenders.

character data: The textual data of an XML document. Character data doesn't include the markup of the document.

character encoding scheme: A method for encoding characters as bit patterns. XML uses the Unicode standard for encoding characters in text, which allows for the 8-bit character encoding scheme, known as *UTF-8,* as well as the 16-bit scheme, known as *UTF-16.* UTF-8 is compatible with plain text, or standard ASCII, while UTF-16 can support a much larger set of characters.

character reference: A method of invoking a character that you can't enter directly via the computer keyboard or other input device. Also referred to as an **escape code.**

child element: *See* **subelement.**

class: A set of objects that share similar properties. A class could be a type of logical structure, such as elements, attributes, comments, or processing instructions. (In reference to documents, *see also* **document class.**)

client: A software module that receives and interprets a set of data from another source — usually a server.

client-side include: An instruction or set of instructions embedded within a document that processes some type of data on or within the client.

combining character: A character that combines with or attaches to the visible form of another character. Combining characters contain most of the diacritics.

comment: A method of including text in a DTD or document that is readable by human eyes but is invisible to an XML application.

conditional section: A set of markup that is either included in or excluded from the logical structure of the DTD, determined by the keyword `INCLUDE` or `IGNORE`, respectively.

content model: A technical description of an element, including its contents.

content particles (cps): The grammar for element content, which describes the allowed types of child elements and the order in which the child elements must appear.

decimal reference: A number consisting of digits 0 through 9, preceded by an ampersand and a pound sign (&#), and immediately followed by a semicolon (;).

declaration: A statement within the DTD that provides a technical instruction for the composition and behavior of a document.

delimiter: A character or sequence of characters that marks the beginning or end of a unit of data.

diacritic: A mark applied or attached to a character to create an entirely different character.

digit: A character within a range of numbers.

document: *See* **XML document.**

document class: A group of documents that conform to the same rules of grammar by being associated with a single DTD.

document element: An element, identified by the document type declaration, containing the content of the entire document. All XML documents must have one, and only one, document element. Also referred to as **root element.**

document entity: An essential entity that serves as the starting point for the XML processor and contains the entire document, including all other entities. Also referred to as **root entity.**

document management system: A computer system that manages and serves a large number of documents, as well as data that is classified in multiple ways.

Document Style Semantics and Specification Language (DSSSL): An international standard (ISO/IEC 10179:1996) for associating processing with SGML documents.

document type declaration: A declaration at the beginning of an XML document that may specify the location for the external DTD subset and/or include the internal DTD subset.

document type definition (DTD): The set of rules that define the instructions for the document. Specifically, a DTD is composed of a set of declarations that determine the element types — including the allowed content and attributes for each element — as well as external entities and notations.

down-conversion: The process of converting a document or set of documents in XML to another format.

DSSSL: *See* **Document Style Semantics and Specification Language.**

DTD: *See* **document type definition.**

EBNF: *See* **Extended Backus-Naur Form.**

editor: An authoring tool used to compose XML DTDs or documents.

element: A logical unit of information.

element content: A content model that allows elements to contain only other elements and not character data.

element-content model: A content model composed of only elements and excluding character data.

element declaration: A declaration that defines and constrains an element.

element type: A particular class of elements, identified by name.

empty element: An element that doesn't contain any content (subelements or character data). An empty element requires only one tag, rather than the pair of start- and end-tags required by nonempty elements.

empty-element tag: The markup tag of an element that doesn't contain any content (subelements or character data). An empty element requires only one tag, rather than the pair of start- and end-tags required by nonempty elements.

encoding declaration: The declaration that defines the character encoding scheme used for a particular text entity.

end-tag: A tag that marks the end of a nonempty element's boundary. An end-tag is the latter half of a start- and end-tag pair.

entity: The data that makes up one virtual storage unit, or a unit of physical structure. Each entity consists of a name, which identifies the entity, and a value, or the content of the entity, which consists of either the data of the entity itself or is a pointer to the data.

entity declaration: A declaration that defines the name of an entity and associates it with a corresponding replacement string or with data that's stored externally and identified by a URL.

entity reference: A pointer within the textual data of an XML document to a previously declared entity. Upon parsing the entity reference, the XML processor must expand and include the corresponding entity.

escape code: *See* **character reference.**

expansion: The process of replacing an entity or character reference with its replacement text.

Extended Backus-Naur Form (EBNF): The notation used in the XML Specification, defining each rule in the grammar as `symbol ::= expression`.

extender: A symbol beyond the previously defined character set being used.

Extensible Markup Language (XML): A World Wide Web Consortium standard and specification for a metalanguage used to define markup languages, document type definitions, or data applications.

Extensible Style Language (XSL): A standard for an XML-compatible style sheet language, proposed by the World Wide Web Consortium.

external DTD subset: A separate file referenced by a document that contains a DTD. An external DTD subset, along with an internal DTD subset (if one exists), makes up a DTD.

external entity: An entity mapped to data located outside its declaration. An external entity may contain either parsed/text or unparsed/binary data.

external identifier: A pointer to a URL. Both the system identifier and the public identifier are external identifiers.

fatal error: The halting of normal XML processing, which is triggered by the violation of a well-formedness constraint dictated by the XML Specification. A validating XML processor may trigger a fatal error upon a violation of a validity constraint as well.

general entity: A parsed entity used within the document content, referenced by the name of the entity beginning with an ampersand (&) and ending with a semicolon (;).

general purpose enumeration: An enumerated type consisting of a set of `NMTOKEN` tokens.

generic identifier (GI): The name assigned to an element type.

GI: *See* **generic identifier.**

grove: A conceptual tree or set of trees composed of classes and subclasses.

helper application: A separate application spawned from the XML application, such as an image-viewer or a video player.

hexadecimal reference: A base-16 number consisting of digits 0 through 9 and/or letters A (or a) through F (or f), preceded by an ampersand, pound sign, and the literal string x (&#x), and immediately followed by a semicolon (;).

HTML: *See* **HyperText Markup Language.**

HyperText Markup Language (HTML): An SGML-based fixed markup language designed for composing and viewing documents on the World Wide Web.

ideographic character: A graphic symbol retained by a single byte of data.

internal DTD subset: A set of declarations in the prolog of a document. The internal DTD subset may contain a pointer to the external DTD subset that, when taken together, form the DTD. Also referred to as **local DTD.**

internal entity: An entity whose value is provided within its declaration. All internal entities are parsed, or composed of textual data, which is delimited by quotes.

intranet: A private or organizational network that uses Internet technology.

letter: A character of any alphabet.

literal data: A quoted string of characters, excluding the double quotes (") or apostrophes (') delimiting the string.

local DTD: See **internal DTD subset.**

logical structure: The rules of how an XML document is organized. Logical structure is composed of declarations, elements, processing instructions, and other instructions that are indicated by explicit markup within the document.

markup: Data within a document that indicates the logical and physical structure of the document.

markup language: A language used to design the markup for a document or class of documents.

metalanguage: A markup-design language from which markup languages can be derived.

mixed content: Document data consisting of character data, optionally interspersed with subelements.

mixed-content declaration: An element declaration specifying mixed content.

name: A token beginning with a letter or an underscore.

name token: A mixture of name characters.

name-value pair: The components of an attribute that are applied to an element.

nest: To lie properly within an element's boundaries. For well-formedness, a set of a start-tag and a corresponding end-tag that delimits a subelement must nest within the set of a start-tag and a corresponding end-tag that marks the element containing the subelement.

nonempty element: An element that contains content — either subelements or character data or both — delimited by a *start-tag* at the beginning of the element and an *end-tag* at the end.

nonvalidating XML processor: An XML processor that checks XML documents for well-formedness but not for validity. A nonvalidating XML processor can ignore information provided in the DTD and process DTD-less documents without a problem.

normalization: The process of massaging the data sent to the XML application.

notation: The format of the data of an external binary entity. A notation could indicate any legitimate file format, such as a BMP image, MPEG video, TXT plain-text file, or PL Perl script. Also, the syntax of the rules of XML grammar. (*See also* **Extended Backus-Naur Form.**)

notation declaration: A declaration that identifies and defines a format for a type of external binary entity.

parameter entity: A parsed entity used only within the DTD, referenced by a name beginning with an ampersand (&) and ending with a semicolon (;).

parseable character data: Data made up of characters and read as text by the XML parser. The moniker for parseable character data is `PCDATA`.

parsed: XML-readable character data, containing the textual content or markup that forms part of an XML document. Also referred to as **text.**

parsed entity: An entity containing parsed data, or text, invoked by the parsed entity reference. Also referred to as **text entity.**

parser: A software module that parses, or reads the data of, an XML document, and checks it for validity or well-formedness. The job of the XML processor overlaps that of the parser. Also referred to as **XML parser.**

physical structure: The set of and arrangement of entities, or physical storage units, that make up an XML document.

PI: *See* **processing instruction.**

PI target: The name that identifies a processing instruction (PI) included within a DTD to an XML application.

predefined entities: A set of five entities escaped by special sequences of code. The predefined entities include the ampersand: &, escaped by the predefined entity `amp`; the less-than sign (or left-angle bracket): <, escaped by the predefined entity `lt`; the greater-than sign (or right-angle bracket): >, escaped by the predefined entity `gt`; the apostrophe (or single quote): ', escaped by the predefined entity `apos`; and the quotation mark (or double quote): ", escaped by the predefined entity `quot`.

prefix operator: A character preceding an expression code that changes the meaning of the expression or indicates a special instruction for it. In XML, the prefix operator (%) specifies that in the external DTD subset a parameter entity may occur in the text at the position where expression unit `a` may occur.

processing instruction (PI): Markup that sends information or an instruction to the XML processor. PIs are not textually part of the XML document.

processor: A software module that reads XML documents, provides access to their content and structure to the XML application, checks for well-formedness and optionally for validity, and reports any errors. An XML processor, or XML-compliant software that includes an XML processor, usually has a parser built into it. For this reason, the terms *parser* and *processor* in relation to XML are often used interchangeably.

prolog: A section of a document that includes the internal DTD subset and that precedes the document element, or the document proper.

property: A technical description of a class.

public identifier: An identifier that provides a public or alternative URL for the location of an external entity.

recursive: Constituting a procedure that repeats itself indefinitely.

replacement text: The content of a parsed entity.

root element: *See* **document element.**

root entity: *See* **document entity.**

rule: A complete statement within the XML Specification that defines the grammar of XML, including the legal syntax and sets of allowed codes or sequences of characters for DTDs and documents, as well as the instructions for XML processors and applications.

server: A software module that sends data and instructions to at least one client.

server-side include (SSI): An instruction or set of instructions embedded within a document that processes some type of data on or within the server.

SGML: *See* **Standard Generalized Markup Language.**

SSI: *See* **server-side include.**

standalone document declaration: A declaration that determines that an XML document doesn't rely on any external sources of information, such as an external DTD or an external parameter entity referenced by the internal DTD subset. This type of XML document is completely self-sufficient; that is, all of its necessary information appears within the document itself.

standalone status: The value of the standalone document declaration. A value of "no" tells the XML processor that external declarations may exist. The standalone status doesn't change regardless of whether references to external entities are included within the internal DTD subset.

Standard Generalized Markup Language (SGML): An International Organization for Standardization (ISO 8879:1986) specification used for defining markup languages. SGML comes first in the chronology of standard markup languages, and so it is the mother tongue of a wide variety of both proprietary and public document types.

start-tag: A tag that marks the start of a nonempty element's boundary. A start-tag is the former half of a start- and end-tag pair.

subelement: An element located within another element. A subelement is the child of the element; conversely, the element is the parent of that subelement. Although a subelement is a child of another element, it's a complete element in and of itself and may contain other elements as well as text. Also referred to as **child element.**

suffix operator: A character following an expression code that changes the meaning of the expression or indicates a special instruction for it. In XML, suffix operators include the question mark (?) for zero or one time that the expression occurs, the plus sign (+) for one or more times, and the asterisk (*) for zero or more times.

syntactic construct: The specific syntax of symbols in XML grammar. Common syntactic constructs include literals, names, and tokens.

system identifier: An identifier that provides a URL for the location of an external entity.

tag: A delimiter that marks an empty element or the beginning or end of a nonempty element within a document.

text: *See* **parsed.**

text entity: *See* **parsed entity.**

token: A label representing distinctive units of information within a rule.

Unicode: An international standard (ISO/IEC 10646-1;1993) used to encode text for computer processing.

Uniform Resource Locator (URL): A standard scheme for accessing an Internet resource.

unparsed: Data consisting of code that isn't XML-encoded. Unparsed data may translate into a graphic image, a sound file, an application, or even a non-XML plain-text file. Also referred to as **binary.**

unparsed entity: An entity containing unparsed data, or binary data, which is invoked by the unparsed entity reference. The content of an unparsed entity can't be parsed by the processor, and it may or may not be text; even if it is text, it may not be XML-encoded text. Also referred to as **binary entity.**

up-conversion: The process of converting a document or set of documents in a non-XML format to XML.

URL: *See* **Uniform Resource Locator.**

valid: The state of an XML document that conforms to all the rules expressed in its DTD.

validating XML processor: An XML processor that checks XML documents for validity, which is a set of additional constraints beyond well-formedness. A validating XML processor, therefore, must be able to read a DTD — and it actually requires the presence of a DTD for validation.

validity constraint: A rule within the XML Specification that dictates validity.

well-formed: The state of an XML document that conforms to all the rules for well-formedness expressed in the XML Specification. Well-formedness includes the presence of a document element that contains any subelements properly nested within it as well as properly declared entity references.

well-formedness constraint: A rule within the XML Specification that dictates well-formedness.

white space: The visibly empty space between characters. White space may include one or more space characters (hexadecimal Unicode character #x20), carriage returns (hexadecimal Unicode character #x9), line feeds (hexadecimal Unicode character #xD), or tabs (hexadecimal Unicode character #xA). White-space characters may combine to form a section of white space.

white-space handling: The treatment of white space by the XML processor.

World Wide Web: A subset of the Internet that uses the Hypertext Transfer Protocol (HTTP) and HTML documents.

XLL: *See* **XML Linking Specification.**

XML: *See* **Extensible Markup Language.**

XML declaration: The first declaration in an XML document that asserts that the document is an XML document and that specifies the version of XML.

XML document: A well-formed document that conforms to the XML Specification.

XML/HTML hybrid system: A document management system, Web site, or intranet that uses both XML and HTML document standards.

XML Linking Specification (XLL): A specification for describing links, or data relationships, between objects within XML, proposed by the World Wide Web Consortium.

XML parser: *See* **parser.**

XML processor: *See* **processor.**

XML Specification: The official rules of grammar for XML as determined and governed by the World Wide Web Consortium.

XSL: *See* **Extensible Style Language.**

Index

Z

Notes

Notes

_____

_____

_____

_____

_____

_____

_____

_____

_____

_____

_____

_____

_____

_____

_____

_____

_____

_____

_____

_____

_____

_____

_____

Discover Dummies Online!

The Dummies Web Site is your fun and friendly online resource for the latest information about ...For Dummies® books and your favorite topics. The Web site is the place to communicate with us, exchange ideas with other ...For Dummies readers, chat with authors, and have fun!

Ten Fun and Useful Things You Can Do at www.dummies.com

1. Win free ...For Dummies books and more!
2. Register your book and be entered in a prize drawing.
3. Meet your favorite authors through the IDG Books Author Chat Series.
4. Exchange helpful information with other ...For Dummies readers.
5. Discover other great ...For Dummies books you must have!
6. Purchase Dummieswear™ exclusively from our Web site.
7. Buy ...For Dummies books online.
8. Talk to us. Make comments, ask questions, get answers!
9. Download free software.
10. Find additional useful resources from authors.

Link directly to these ten
fun and useful things at
http://www.dummies.com/10useful

For other technology titles from IDG Books Worldwide, go to
www.idgbooks.com

Not on the Web yet? It's easy to get started with Dummies 101®: The Internet For Windows® 95 or The Internet For Dummies®, 5th Edition, at local retailers everywhere.

Find other ...For Dummies books on these topics:

Business • Career • Databases • Food & Beverage • Games • Gardening • Graphics
Hardware • Health & Fitness • Internet and the World Wide Web • Networking • Office Suites
Operating Systems • Personal Finance • Pets • Programming • Recreation • Sports
Spreadsheets • Teacher Resources • Test Prep • Word Processing

IDG BOOKS WORLDWIDE BOOK REGISTRATION

Register
This Book
and Win!

We want to hear from you!

Visit **http://my2cents.dummies.com** to register this book and tell us how you liked it!

- Get entered in our monthly prize giveaway.

- Give us feedback about this book — tell us what you like best, what you like least, or maybe what you'd like to ask the author and us to change!

- Let us know any other *...For Dummies*® topics that interest you.

Your feedback helps us determine what books to publish, tells us what coverage to add as we revise our books, and lets us know whether we're meeting your needs as a *...For Dummies* reader. You're our most valuable resource, and what you have to say is important to us!

Not on the Web yet? It's easy to get started with *Dummies 101*®: *The Internet For Windows*® *95* or *The Internet For Dummies*,® 5th Edition, at local retailers everywhere.

Or let us know what you think by sending us a letter at the following address:

...For Dummies Book Registration
Dummies Press
7260 Shadeland Station, Suite 100
Indianapolis, IN 46256-3945
Fax 317-596-5498

BUSINESS AND
GENERAL
REFERENCE
BOOK SERIES
FROM IDG

COMPUTER
BOOK SERIES
FROM IDG